"Calvin Eng draws on traditional Cantonese techniques and the mixing of Cantonese and American flavors that reflect our own experience. And he does it with a verve and creativity that make us want to run to the kitchen and start cooking!"
—SARAH, KAITLIN, BILL, and JUDY LEUNG, *New York Times* bestselling authors of *The Woks of Life: Recipes to Know and Love from a Chinese American Family*

"*Salt Sugar MSG* is a triumphant celebration of home and family, showcasing Calvin's inventive approach to cooking that breathes new life into classic Cantonese dishes. Most of all, the book perfectly captures the bold spirit and generosity of Cantonese American cooking."
—HETTY LUI MCKINNON, food writer and James Beard Award–winning author of five cookbooks

"So much of Chef Eng's book resonates with my own experience as an immigrant from Canton. Thoughtful, personal, and joyful, it's a wonderful read as well as a handy guide in the kitchen."
—CHEF MARTIN YAN, host of *Yan Can Cook* on PBS

"In this debut cookbook, Brooklyn-born chef Calvin Eng delightfully weaves stories of growing up in New York's Chinatown eating and learning to cook his mother's humble Toisan dishes with his culinary path to develop his own distinct style, adding a fresh twist to Cantonese classics. With his inventive fusion of modern and traditional ingredients—what he affectionately calls a 'mishmash of identities'—Eng contributes a vibrant chapter to the ever-evolving narrative of multicultural American cuisine."
—GRACE YOUNG, James Beard Award–winning author of *Stir-Frying to the Sky's Edge*

"This book is more than just breaking the misrepresentation of MSG—it's about the delicious places that live in between American and Chinese traditions."
—BRANDON JEW, executive chef and owner of Mister Jiu's and author of James Beard Award–winning *Mister Jiu's in Chinatown*

"Everything from the title, the mouthwatering recipes, the stunning photography, and warm writing feels like a homecoming. *Salt Sugar MSG* is an important cookbook that will add so much inspiration, nostalgia, and flavor to your kitchen."
—KRISTINA CHO, James Beard Award–winning cookbook author of *Mooncakes & Milk Bread* and *Chinese Enough*

"*Salt Sugar MSG* reads like a reflection of my own life experiences as a Chinese American. The writing spoke so genuinely to what life was like for so many of us that it felt like Calvin was at times telling *the* story as opposed to just his own. The recipes are as effortlessly rooted in identity as they are effortlessly clever and full of a love of eating."
—JON KUNG, author of *Kung Food*

"As a third-culture kid myself, growing up between worlds, I've always felt a recognition and kinship with Calvin and his food. His 'not-traditional-but-personal' mashups and twists on Canto classics are approachable yet revelatory, pushing Chinese cuisine further within our collective culture."
—JING GAO, founder and CEO of Fly By Jing, author of James Beard Award–winning *The Book of Sichuan Chili Crisp*

CALVIN ENG *with* PHOEBE MELNICK

SALT
SUGAR
MSG

RECIPES *and* STORIES
FROM A CANTONESE AMERICAN HOME

PHOTOGRAPHS BY ALEX LAU

CLARKSON POTTER/PUBLISHERS
NEW YORK

For our sweet little boy, Levi

INTRODUCTION
9

BUILDING BLOCKS
OF CANTONESE
AMERICAN COOKING
14

EQUIPMENT LIST
39

HOW TO BECOME
THE MOST EFFICIENT
HOME COOK
(From a Restaurant Cook)
44

1
BREAKFAST
49

2
SNACKS
77

3
VEGETABLES
103

4
RICE
131

5
NOODLES
157

6
MEATS
185

7
SEAFOOD
217

8
SWEETS
237

ACKNOWLEDGMENTS
263

INDEX
267

INTRODUCTION

This is not a Cantonese cookbook.
Not in the traditional sense, at least.

I grew up surrounded by a family chitchatting in a seamless mix of Toisanese and English, with bits of Cantonese scattered throughout, never speaking in the same language for more than a few words. Honestly, my Toisanese has always been significantly better than my Cantonese. It's a dying dialect that often wins me an extra egg tart from the ladies behind the counter at my favorite bakery—a hint of street cred with the old crowd—a slow, sneaky smile. They aren't used to hearing anyone under the age of fifty speak it. But everyone in my family does. It's the dialect of Toisan, a county in the Guangdong Province in southeast China—the place where both sides of my family originated.

My mom was barely thirteen years old when she immigrated to New York with her sister and brother. She met her dad for the very first time when they landed in the city. He had moved to Manhattan's Chinatown in the hope that one day the whole family would be able to join him before she was even born. It took a bit longer than anyone had anticipated, but my mom, her parents, and her two siblings settled into a one-bedroom apartment on the center of Bayard Street at the heart of the neighborhood. It was impossibly tiny; a clawfoot bathtub filled the middle of the kitchen and a broken oven stood in the corner, serving only as extra storage. My mom and her sister slept in a bunk bed, a somewhat sturdy contraption my grandfather pulled together to squish as many people as possible into one bedroom. Her brother slept in the kitchen on a pull-out cot that was tucked away the second his eyes opened each morning. Anything to keep the family together under one roof. My grandparents stayed in that place for over fifty years. They made Chinatown their home.

My mom lived on Bayard Street until she met my father when she was twenty-four. Almost a decade after moving to the States. When they married, he whisked her away to south Brooklyn, to the neighborhood his family now lived in after moving from those same tiny villages in southern China her family had once called home. But weekend after weekend, she

9

dutifully and diligently returned to Chinatown. She dropped in to run errands for my grandparents and bring them groceries, to take them to doctors' appointments and occasionally out to lunch. For years, she took my older sister around the neighborhood with her, and eventually, when I was old enough, she dragged me along too. I'd sit curled up on the couch, coloring on pads of paper while my mom, aunt, and grandma caught up on the weekly gossip. More often than not, though, they spent those hours sitting in silence, enjoying their time together again under the same roof.

It's embarrassing to admit now, but I hated that apartment when I was younger. That space and those blocks felt like the physical representation of everything that made me different, a constant reminder of my not-so-traditional American upbringing. Different from the kids at school whose moms packed them buttered noodles and peanut butter and jelly for lunch. Now I desperately miss it all. The space where I learned to play mahjong with my grandma on the tiny foldout table. The kitchen I snacked on fresh rice rolls stuffed with slivers of marinated steak drenched in sweet soy with my grandfather and fried bow ties dripping in a sticky honey syrup with my aunt. The early weekend mornings I chased my mom up and down and all around Chinatown while she grocery shopped, navigating the sidewalks cluttered with fruit stalls as she dodged aunties who lugged their rolling-book-bags-turned-shopping-carts with ease. The neighborhood lined with restaurants we packed into weekend after weekend, celebrating birthdays and weddings, new lives and those who were no longer with us. Celebrating each other. Celebrating family.

That's the funny thing about growing up. Sometimes you never truly understand how lucky and full your life is until you get a little older—until you have a little distance. I was so envious of those "more American" kids for years, practically up until I hit my twenties. By then, I had graduated from culinary school and taken a job at a restaurant on the edge of Chinatown. Suddenly I found myself hand-shopping for fresh vegetables and jars of condiments the way my mom had taught me years before, speaking Toisanese in the shops I had grown up frequenting, strolling down the blocks my grandparents had once roamed daily. Now, I walked those streets for inspiration rather than obligation, for appreciation rather than resentment.

A few years later, that same inspiration morphed into something more concrete: a restaurant—my restaurant, which I named Bonnie's in honor of the American name my aunt chose for my mom when they first moved to New York City from Hong Kong. A restaurant for kids who grew up a little confused about their identities and where they fit into the world, like me. A restaurant for kids who are now proud of their heritage, like me. A restaurant dedicated to my Cantonese roots and my American upbringing.

And a year or so later, that same appreciation morphed into something more: a cookbook—this cookbook, stuffed with recipes that are deeply rooted in classic Cantonese flavors. Subtle, savory sauces and salty, preserved bites. Steaming trays of fresh fresh seafood served alongside bowls of fluffy jasmine rice. Salt, sugar, MSG and ginger, garlic, scallion.

Calvin and Bonnie in the backyard of their Brooklyn home.

Suey Chew in the Bayard Street Apartment.

INTRODUCTION

A book filled with techniques—stir-frying and steaming, velveting meats and sizzling hot oils—from the conventional Cantonese kitchen. A book packed with dishes influenced by more than just my mom's kitchen in Brooklyn and the roast meat shops lining the blocks of Chinatown, the banquet halls and dim sum parlors—dishes that dip into the melting pot that is New York City.

Each recipe in this book serves a purpose, from highlighting an essential Cantonese technique to expanding on a flavor or ingredient. Some of the cooking stays relatively true to the classics, minus a few tweaks here and there. The Sizzling Steamed Fish with Seasoned Soy Sauce (page 218) is practically the textbook definition of homey Cantonese cooking. A whole fish, tossed in a tray with a few slivers of ginger and then lightly steamed, finished with a hit of seasoned soy and a drizzle of sizzling hot oil to caramelize the fresh ginger and scallions scattered over top. This was a dish my mom made twice if not three times a week—a weeknight staple from my childhood that still excites and inspires me, that I crave and think about on the regular.

Other recipes don't look especially Cantonese but certainly taste that way. Take the recipe for BLT Fried Rice (page 140). Heavily inspired by a regular old BLT, this fried rice really *is* an amalgamation of Cantonese and American flavors and techniques. Chunks of smoky, thick-cut American bacon stud this ultra-classic Cantonese-style fried rice. Seasoned simply with salt, sugar, and MSG and plumped up in the leftover bacon grease, the glistening grains of rice are the star of the show. There's no drizzle of soy sauce to stain the rice at the end. Instead it's finished with just a handful of shredded lettuce and some juicy, fresh, acidic tomatoes, and a squeeze of Kewpie mayo to tie it all together. It's a true mishmash of identities—kind of like me. I'm not cooking with Cantonese flavors as some sort of gimmick. I've always thought of my cooking as a natural evolution from the food I grew up eating: a little bit of Americana mixed into Cantonese classics along with a heavy dash of nostalgia.

As a result, Salt Sugar MSG could never
be a traditional Cantonese cookbook.
It always had to be Cantonese American.

BUILDING BLOCKS OF CANTONESE AMERICAN COOKING

The most important trio in Cantonese cooking is salt, sugar, and MSG.

Of course there's also the holy trinity—the trifecta of ginger, garlic, and scallion—that makes up the Chinese equivalent of the traditional French mirepoix of onion, carrot, and celery. Fresh ginger offers a warm, spicy (but not fiery) taste, while cooked-down garlic lends buttery sweetness. Scallions have a mild, oniony flavor that only heightens over heat and a fresh, crisp bite when kept raw and sprinkled over a finished dish. These three delicate aromatics perfume a dish throughout, from the very beginning to the very end.

But when it comes to salt, sugar, and MSG, you don't have to think about these three components so literally.

The salt in a dish could come from soy sauce or fish sauce; the sugar from fruit, honey, maple syrup, or sweetened condensed milk; the MSG from Parmesan, tomatoes, mushrooms, or any preserved or fermented product. Whenever I'm cooking, I look for ingredients that can add pops of salt or umami in a dish—products like fermented black soybeans or ham yue (Cantonese salted preserved fish)—so every bite is varied. While each ingredient can stand on its own, mixed together you have a seasoning powerhouse.

SALT

I love salt. I love it to the point that I've been told I have a heavy hand with it, especially by my mom. But salt both concentrates flavor and deepens flavor. It's integral not only to savory food but to sweets too. Without salt, food tastes flat and bland. When I call for salt in this trifecta, it's always kosher salt. The bigger granules are easy to pinch between your fingers and even easier to disperse uniformly when seasoning. Of the two major kosher salt brands occupying most grocery-store shelves, I reach for Diamond Crystal. This is the salt I used to develop and test all the recipes in this book.

SUGAR

Specifically, I mean regular old granulated white sugar, which balances everything out. Sugar can intensify the overall taste of a dish, but it can also soften overly sour or bitter notes and level out the salt in a dish.

MSG

This is the punch of umami that makes a dish—that makes you salivate, that keeps you coming back for more. I don't add MSG to recipes for the controversial shock factor. I truly believe the seasoning adds something you can't achieve with just salt and sugar alone. Naturally occurring in cheeses and dried seafood, MSG has quite the stigmatized history. In 1968, the *New England Journal of Medicine* published a letter written by Dr. Robert Ho Man Kwok. He wrote of the numbness, headaches, and heart palpitations he personally experienced after eating Chinese food seasoned with monosodium glutamate, or MSG, symptoms that were soon dubbed "Chinese restaurant syndrome." Chinese restaurant owners shied away from the seasoning due to the backlash, and No MSG symbols popped up on their menus. In recent years, the hate toward MSG has lessened as health experts have endorsed the seasoning's safety, but there is still a ways to go in removing the unfortunate xenophobic undertones attached to the name. As a lover and user of MSG on a massive scale, I choose to proudly advertise my use of it not only in the dishes on my menu at Bonnie's but also in a heart-shaped tattoo on the back of my arm. It just makes food taste good.

Working together, these six ingredients are the building blocks to just about every sauce or condiment, every stir-fry, every stew or braise, every marinade.

These are the essential flavors of Cantonese American food.

WHAT TO BUY

Like salt, sugar, and MSG, store-bought sauces and condiments are fundamental to Cantonese cooking. Every Chinese mom is loyal to specific brands, so much so that moms often pass that loyalty down to their children. Over the years, I've curated my ideal pantry shelf: some are old mainstays, like my mom's favorite brand of shrimp paste, but others I've found through trial and error, conversations with friends, and hours spent in the aisles of Chinatown grocery shops. I'm constantly stopping by shops to buy condiments and sauces, pickled things and dried things, cans and jars to lug home. I'm always testing out new brands to add to my personal pantry. It's honestly to the point that we've actually run out of shelf space in our tiny apartment.

When you start building out your pantry to cook through this book, I recommend hitting your local Asian grocery store to shop. Every bottle of hoisin and jar of *fuyu* taste a little different, depending on the brand, so listed on the next pages are some of the specific ones I used to develop the recipes in this book. If you don't happen to live near a Chinatown or if your neighborhood doesn't have an Asian grocer nearby to peruse, you can buy a lot of these ingredients online. Umamicart is a wonderful website that ships sauces and condiments, flours and bags of rice, fruits and veggies, fresh *ho fun* noodles and even fun snacky bites straight to your door. Amazon is always a great resource, too, but of course it's always preferable if you can source these ingredients from local Asian vendors to support them.

CANTONESE CHARCUTERIE
Cured, salty bites of meat, Cantonese charcuterie is easy to find at any Asian supermarket. The two types I always have on hand are *lap cheong* (Chinese sausage links) and *lap yuk* (cured Chinese bacon). Both are sweet and salty pork products that are preserved by air-drying, creating a concentrated depth of flavor. Growing up, my mom would simply toss a few links of sausage or slices of bacon into a pot of uncooked rice to steam together; the fat would melt out of the cured pork, leaving chewy bites while coating the grains until they glistened.

DRIED SEAFOOD
Dried shrimp, scallops, and anchovies are deeply concentrated seafood umami bombs. I keep a stash in my fridge (to prolong the shelf life) to use as last-minute flavor boosters. Dried shrimp has a pungent, in-your-face shrimp taste, great for flavoring chili oil (page 36) or reinforcing a shrimpy flavor in broth for wontons (page 170). Dried scallops and anchovies bring a subtle yet deep, sweet, seafoody flavor to XO sauce (page 37). The scallops are definitely a pricier pantry staple, but it makes sense when you think about how they are processed. Scallops are expensive when they're fresh, but the time and effort it takes to sun dry them only adds value and flavor. The bigger pieces of dried shrimp, scallops, and anchovies will always be sweeter and more fragrant, but their smaller counterparts are just as delicious, and a little goes a long way. You'll often find packages of dried seafood stocked by the refrigerator aisle in Asian grocery stores, or sold by the pound in large glass jars in specialty shops in Chinatown, but you can also easily order online.

DRIED SHIITAKE MUSHROOMS
Shiitakes, like fresh seafood, have that same umami flavor that intensifies dramatically with drying. There are a ton of dried mushrooms on the market, but the Cantonese love sweet and earthy shiitakes most. Look for packages filled with thick, mushrooms with curved caps that yield the richest flavor. Pop them into stocks and soups to build a rich, dark broth and a meaty, savory quality without having to use any meat. Reconstitute the fungi in a bowl of water before chopping and folding them into pork and chive filling for dumplings (page 94) .

EVAPORATED MILK

Easy to find in any baking aisle, shelf-stable cans of evaporated milk are a mainstay in Chinese households across the country. Stirred into mugs of Milk Tea (page 74) or *yeun yeung* (page 74) and whisked into a creamy dessert soup (page 242) and silky sweetened egg custard (page 252), evaporated milk is naturally richer but not much sweeter than your average glass of milk and makes for a great substitution. Prior to canning, milk is heated to remove about 60 percent of the water, leaving an almost heavy cream–like texture behind. Once opened, the cans of milk can last in the fridge for up to week.

FERMENTED BLACK SOYBEANS

These black soybeans, not to be confused with the Western staple black beans, are sun-dried to the point that they look like shriveled raisins, then coated in salt and left to ferment. They have a lightly sweet smell but taste bitter and briny and, of course, very salty. If you find the soybeans too salty, you can soak them in a bowl of cold water and then rinse them thoroughly before cooking with them. I use them as the base for my Black Bean Garlic Sauce (page 28) that is great over clams (page 227) or tofu (page 201). Some brands, like Yang Jiang, are preserved with ginger for a subtle spicy, floral bite, but a dish will be just as tasty without if you can't find this specific brand on the shelves at your local Asian grocery store.

Brand recommendation: Yang Jiang

FRIED GARLIC

Think big containers of minced garlic cloves that have been fried until crispy and lightly golden. You could always do this yourself at home, but that requires blanching and frying and patience when the store-bought product is consistently good every time. Straight out of the jar, it's extremely strong and pungent. I like to treat it as a seasoning in dressings and sauces or blitz it up to use in spice mixes (page 34). Try to find the jars without any bits of garlic skin. You don't want to pay for skins that you'll just have to pick out and toss.

Brand recommendation: Golden Buffalo

FRIED SHALLOTS

Oftentimes labeled fried red onions, fried shallots are the Asian equivalent of French's Crispy Fried Onions. Great as a garnish for extra crunchy flavor, I often treat fried shallots similarly to fried garlic to make the most out of the sweet, oniony bite.

Brand recommendation: Wangderm

FUYU / FERMENTED BEAN CURD

These small cubes of fermented tofu, also known as bean curd, pack a lot of blue-cheesy flavor in a small bite. Stuffed into glass jars filled with brining liquid, this tofu is salty and soft and delicate. You will often find two different styles of *fuyu* in the condiment aisle, the plain "white" version or one with chili added. I only cook with the *fuyu* with chili; it adds a subtle kiss of heat that's not too overpowering. My mom used to toss cubes of *fuyu* along with garlic in the wok to stir-fry vegetables, but I like to use the back of a spoon or spatula to smoosh the soft cubes into room-temperature unsalted butter to mellow out the potent saltiness while still maintaining the strong briny, savory notes.

Brand recommendation: Hwang Ryh Shiang

HAM YUE / SALTED PRESERVED FISH

This salted preserved fish is the Cantonese equivalent of good salty, fatty anchovies. Typically made from yellow croaker, the fresh fish is gutted but left whole, aggressively salted inside and out to remove as much moisture as possible, and then left to dry under the beating sun. I'll be the first to say it's an acquired taste and smell. You would never eat this straight out of the packaging, as the dehydrated fish is extremely salty and exceptionally fishy. It must be steamed to rehydrate it back to life before using in a dish. The fish softens in the steamer, releasing its naturally fragrant oils and transforming into an entirely different yet still very salty product. From there, you can simply eat it served over a bowl of steamed jasmine rice (page 136) for a homey Cantonese classic or mince it up and fold it into fatty pork for a mouthwatering steamed salted fish and pork patty (page 188). I buy my *ham yue* from a little shop in Chinatown that specializes in dried seafood. Big Asian markets stock it in the dried seafood aisle.

HOISIN SAUCE

Hoisin is a super-thick, dark-brown paste made from fermented soybeans thickened by sweet potato or wheat starch. Both sweet and savory, the sauce is delicious whisked into a marinade and then rubbed onto roast chicken (page 210) or brushed onto a slab of *cha siu* (page 212), or stirred into buttery noodles for the kiddos (page 158).

Brand recommendation: Koon Chun

HOT MUSTARD POWDER

Think wasabi. Think horseradish. Think nose-tingling, sneeze-inducing, sinus-clearing heat. Hot mustard is the Cantonese equivalent of that. Buy it in powdered form to mix with water and maybe a splash of rice vinegar so you can control the thickness and heat. It's great as a dipping sauce for pigs in a blanket (page 96) and Pomegranate Molasses Cha Siu (page 212) or just spread on a regular old deli meat sandwich. Just remember, this spread is potent.

Brand recommendation: S&B Oriental

KEWPIE MAYONNAISE

I grew up in a Hellmann's mayonnaise family because that's what Costco sold in massive packs meant to last a whole year. It wasn't until later in life that I dabbled in new mayos. A family friend casually told me about this amazing mayo they use for their shrimp and walnuts, and suddenly it became a staple in our house. It's tangier and sweeter than regular mayo, with a hit of umami from MSG too.

Brand recommendation: Kewpie

LIGHT AND DARK SOY SAUCES

There are a few types of soy sauce on the market, but the two you'll most commonly find in the following chapters are light and dark. In the simplest terms, they serve two different purposes in a recipe: light soy sauce is used for salt and dark soy sauce is used for color. If you happen to have only one bottle of soy on hand, they are interchangeable for most dishes in this book, but know it's not a perfect one-to-one swap. If a recipe calls for dark soy sauce and you have only light, use a little less to avoid oversalting your dish. Light and dark soy sauces are fermented for different lengths of time, which accounts for the flavor variance. Light soy is fermented less than dark, leaving it with a more powerful, fresh flavor, while longer fermentation gives dark soy a more rounded, mellow flavor. To understand the distinctions, I recommend picking up a bottle of each and sampling them side by side for a fun taste test.

Brand recommendation: Pearl River Bridge

MSG

MSG makes everything taste better. It's not a cheat or a shortcut. It simply enhances a dish. It brings out the depth in a broth that has simmered away for hours (page 29), the savoriness in a steamed egg custard (page 122), or the sweetness in a caramel sauce (page 240). Find it at any Western or Asian supermarket or online and leave it out on your countertop next to your salt cellar and pinch pot of sugar to season anything and everything.

Brand recommendation: Ajinomoto

OILS

Neutral oil and olive oil—these are the two cooking oils you'll see in this cookbook. If a recipe calls for neutral oil, I typically like grapeseed best (and often specifically call it out), but vegetable, canola, and soybean are all perfectly fine. If a recipe calls for olive oil, it's not a typo. I rarely cook with extra-virgin olive oil. I reserve that richer, more full-bodied oil for finishing dishes and for stirring into vinegary, marinated bites. Regular olive oil has a higher smoke point than extra virgin, and neutral oils have even higher smoke points, which is especially important in Cantonese cuisine where a lot of high-heat cooking is done.

OYSTER SAUCE

My mom puts this stuff in every single marinade, stir-fry, and dipping sauce. It makes everything infinitely more tasty. Surprisingly, umami-forward oyster sauce barely tastes like the oyster extracts it's made from. This dark brown sauce adds flavor, body, and color to any dish you stir it into. There are also phenomenal vegetarian oyster sauces on the market made from mushrooms rather than seafood which are equally delicious whether you're vegan, shellfish avoidant, or just interested in stocking your pantry to the fullest.

Brand recommendations: Lee Kum Kee oyster sauce, Wan Ja Shan vegan mushroom oyster sauce

PICKLED MUSTARD GREENS

There is little acid in Cantonese food, so I like to lean on the sour notes from pickled mustard greens (sometimes labeled pickled sour mustard) and their briny liquid to use in sauces, condiments, and stir-fries. Made from large heads of mustard greens with meaty stalks, the greens are often blanched before brining to maintain their crunchy, crisp bite and vibrant color. I like to rinse and soak the heads of greens in cold water for about 30 minutes to remove some of the pungent brine that lingers, as I personally find it too overpowering in my cooking.

SALTED RADISH

Salted radish—sometimes called preserved radish, sweet radish, or salted turnip—is a traditional style of pickle made from daikon radish. A lot of varieties of salted radish are out there. Some are sweet, some are salty, and some are even spicy. Depending on the brand you purchase, you can have a very different end product. Salted radish is relatively inexpensive, so buy a few bags to find your ideal balance of salty, sweet, and spicy. These salted and preserved strips have an amazing crunch, and I love to eat them straight from the bag. I have a high salt tolerance, so people tend to give me a weird look when I pop them like candy. I like to chop up the strips into a fine dice to mimic a meaty texture and flavor in stir-fried vegetables, crispy turnip cakes (page 118), or warm potato salad dripping in XO sauce (page 37).

Brand recommendation: Man Chong Loong

SHAOXING WINE

Made from fermented rice (but not a rice vinegar) and small traces of wheat, this amber-colored Chinese cooking wine is a pantry essential for deglazing and adding a hint of sweetness and fragrance to a dish. The quality of Shaoxing wine can vary drastically. The higher-quality aged wines can be used in cocktails, but there's no need to spend that kind of money for cooking purposes. I'm not loyal to any specific brands when it comes to Shaoxing cooking wines, so test out a few and find your favorite. There aren't any Western pantry substitutions for this flavor—dry cooking sake is probably your best bit in a pinch—so definitely snag a bottle.

SHRIMP PASTE

This little jar of crushed, salted, and fermented shrimp adds lots of fun flavor to a dish. It's potent. It's strong. And it's definitely an acquired taste and smell. I crave it so very much. I don't like using the word *funky* to describe a flavor, but that's what shrimp paste (sometimes labeled as shrimp sauce) is. It's pure funky, salty goodness that's used frequently in many Southeast Asian dishes beyond Cantonese food. Fry off a dollop of this paste in a splash of neutral oil to ramp up any basic stir-fried vegetables, smear it into butter and spread it on roasted cabbage (page 114), or slather it on leftover crispy pork from the roast meat shop and steam until just warmed through for a totally new dish. That was my grandma's favorite way to eat shrimp paste.

Brand recommendation: Lee Kum Kee

SWEETENED CONDENSED MILK

Sweetened condensed milk is a near-perfect ingredient. This canned dairy product, which you can find in the baking aisle of any grocery store, has a much thicker viscosity than evaporated milk and an added bit of sugar. But it similarly has a good amount of the water removed, which yields the smoothest texture for drizzling. It adds a richness and sweetness to baked goods or to a cup of coffee or Milk Tea (page 74) and can keep for up to a week in your fridge after opening.

TINNED DACE FISH

I grew up on this stuff, eating it right out of the can with a bowl of jasmine rice on the side. Like any tinned fish, it's seasoned and preserved, so all you really need is a fork. The little dace fish are fried off before preserving, so all the bones have softened to the point of being edible. Look for the cans with salted black beans mixed in. The beans add a big pop of salt and a fun textural component to every bite.

Brand recommendation: Pearl River Bridge

TOASTED SESAME OIL

There are two types of sesame oil you'll come across on store shelves: toasted and untoasted. I always have a bottle of toasted oil on hand to use for finishing rather than cooking, as it has a very low smoke point. Open a bottle, and you will instantly perfume your whole kitchen with a nutty, toasty scent. Most recipes call for only a tablespoon or two, so grab a smaller bottle and stash it in a cool, dark place so you don't waste any. Like most oils, it can go rancid if it sits too long.

Brand recommendation: Kadoya

WHITE PEPPER

This is what makes Chinese food really taste like Chinese food. If you're ever wondering why the food you make at home just doesn't taste as good as the restaurant stuff, it's because you probably aren't using white pepper. Black and white peppercorns both come from the same plant, but white peppercorns are fermented and dried before removing the outer layer, which results in a more complex, floral bite. You can buy ground white pepper, but I always buy whole peppercorns, toast them in a dry pan until fragrant (but not burned), and grind as needed. (If you want to maximize your spices, grind and toast them yourself.)

1. BLACK BEAN GARLIC SAUCE
2. CANTONESE CHICKEN BROTH
3. CHINESE HOT MUSTARD
4. GREEN CHILI GINGER SCALLION SAUCE

1.

BLACK BEAN GARLIC SAUCE

MAKES 1½ CUPS

¼ cup neutral oil, preferably grapeseed

4 scallions, sliced

10 garlic cloves, minced

2 tablespoons minced ginger

¼ cup fermented black soybeans, minced

2 tablespoons sugar

2 tablespoons Shaoxing wine

2 cups Cantonese Chicken Broth (page 29), low-sodium chicken broth, or water

½ cup plus 2 tablespoons dark soy sauce

2 tablespoons cornstarch

2 tablespoons water

2 teaspoons toasted sesame oil

This is a super-savory sauce made from fermented black soybeans. There are always a few jars of the premade stuff in the grocery aisle to check out. Those are totally fine in a pinch, but they're often packed in too much oil for my taste. I like to make my own sauce so I can tailor it with things I already have in my pantry. On their own, fermented black soybeans can be very salty to the point of being too salty, but the combo of chicken broth and cooked-down garlic really helps to mellow out that aggressive edge while still allowing the fermented flavor to sing. Use this sauce as the base for Steamed Silken Tofu with Beefy Black Bean Garlic Sauce (page 201) or Clams with Black Bean Garlic Sauce (page 227).

1. In a medium pot, heat the neutral oil over medium heat. Add the scallions, garlic, and ginger and sweat the aromatics in the oil, stirring often with about 5 minutes. Add the soybeans and sugar and continue to cook, stirring occasionally, until the soybeans start to soften and break down, about 2 minutes.

2. Add the wine and deglaze the pot, using the rubber spatula to scrape up all the delicious browned bits on the bottom of the pot and stir those flavorful pieces back into the sauce. Simmer until the black beans continue to soften and break down, about 3 minutes.

3. Pour in the broth and soy sauce. Raise the heat to high and bring the sauce to a boil. While the sauce comes to a boil, make a slurry in a small bowl by mixing together the cornstarch and water until smooth. When the sauce is boiling, pour in the slurry around the edge of the pot and stir with the rubber spatula to mix the slurry into the sauce. You should notice the sauce begin to thicken. Let the sauce come back to a boil for about 10 seconds to activate the thickening power of the cornstarch, then remove from the heat.

4. Drizzle in the sesame oil and stir to incorporate. Allow the sauce to cool completely, then store in an airtight container in the fridge for up to 1 week.

2. CANTONESE CHICKEN BROTH

MAKES 3 TO 4 QUARTS

1 (4-pound) whole chicken

1 bunch scallions, cut crosswise into thirds and smashed with the side of a knife

1 head garlic, cloves separated and smashed (no need to peel)

1 (3-inch) piece ginger, sliced into 8 even pieces

1 cup Shaoxing wine

5 quarts cold water

Whenever I'm making a recipe that calls for water, I always swap in this chicken broth. I don't call for salt in this broth, so it won't overpower any dish as a sub for water, but it will pack a lot of natural umami and sweetness (and health!) from the chicken, its collagen, and the OG Chinese trinity. I like to season it with dried shrimp or shrimp shells before serving over a bowl of Shrimp and Pork Wonton Soup (page 170) or use it as the base for a soup like Cantonese Minestrone (page 128). But if you'd like to just sip the broth, jazz it up with a pinch of salt and MSG. And if you hate waste as much as my mom and aunt, you could snack on the chicken from the broth. Just know that it will be dry.

1. In a large (10- to 12-quart) pot, combine the chicken, scallions, garlic, ginger, wine, and water. Bring the mixture to a boil over high heat.

2. Once the mixture is boiling, reduce the heat to medium-low and simmer gently, uncovered, for 6 hours. Check every hour or so to make sure the liquid is still just simmering. If you notice any scum or foam floating on the top, grab a large spoon and skim off those impurities to ensure a clean, clear broth. After 6 hours, the liquid should have reduced by about 25 percent, and the wonderful smell of chicken will be wafting through the house.

3. Using tongs, pull the chicken and aromatics out of the pot. Discard the aromatics and set the chicken aside for snacking, if you like. Pass the broth through a fine-mesh strainer. Let the broth cool down to room temperature, then store in airtight containers in the fridge for up to 3 days, or in the freezer for up to 2 months.

3.

CHINESE
HOT MUSTARD

MAKES 2 CUPS

1 cup rice vinegar

½ cup water

6 tablespoons hot mustard
powder

1 teaspoon kosher salt

1 teaspoon MSG

This is a great condiment to have in your back pocket, another mustard to store in your fridge door. Think of this recipe as a loose guideline: try it out once as is, then you can play with the ratios to tailor it to your taste buds. If you like it a little tarter, add more rice vinegar and less water; if you want a hint of sweetness, try a squeeze of honey (page 97). I think the heat makes for a really fun eating experience, as the spice tingles away in your nose rather than your tongue and throat. Serve with Piggies in Scallion Milk Bread Blankets (page 96) and Pomegranate Molasses Cha Siu (page 212), or slather on sandwiches for a nice hit of heat in your nostrils.

1. In a medium bowl, whisk together the vinegar, water, mustard powder, salt, and MSG until smooth. Store in an airtight container in the fridge for up to 2 weeks.

4.

GREEN CHILI GINGER SCALLION SAUCE

MAKES 3 CUPS

½ cup drained and coarsely chopped pickled mustard greens

½ cup finely minced garlic

½ cup finely minced ginger

½ cup thinly sliced scallions

½ small Italian long hot green chili or serrano chili, seeded and finely diced

1 tablespoon kosher salt

1 tablespoon sugar

1 tablespoon MSG

1 cup neutral oil, preferably grapeseed

A fair number of Western sauces include raw neutral or olive oil to create a luxurious flavor and mouthfeel. But in Cantonese cuisine, we use sizzling-hot oil. We gently heat oil to a specific temperature, changing the flavor notes of the oil before pulling it from the heat and pouring it over a bowl of aromatics or a steamed fish (page 218) topped with ginger and scallion to lightly sizzle and fry away. It's a technique that quickly infuses the oil as it gently cooks the raw bite out of the aromatics and also releases the greatest amount of flavor and aroma. This not-so-traditional ginger scallion sauce is just one application of the hot-oil technique (I love to use it for the Shrimp Chili Oil on page 36), but you can get creative with what you sizzle. Just remember to use a neutral oil with a high smoke point and remove it from the heat the moment you see that first wisp of smoke. Serve this sauce over QQ's Poached Chicken (page 206), stir it into the tartar sauce that accompanies the shrimp sticks (page 88), or eat it over a bowl of steamed jasmine rice.

1. Fill a medium bowl with water, add the mustard greens, and let soak for 30 minutes. Drain the mustard greens and discard the soaking liquid. Wrap the greens in a paper towel and squeeze out any residual water. Set aside.

2. In a medium heatproof bowl, combine the garlic, ginger, scallions, chili, salt, sugar, and MSG and mix well.

3. In a small pot, heat the oil over medium heat to 350°F, then remove the pot from the heat. Gently pour the hot oil over the aromatics and stir. Be extra careful as you work, as the oil can bubble up from all the moisture in the garlic, ginger, and scallions. Allow the ingredients to cool slightly, about 10 minutes, then fold in the mustard greens. Store in an airtight container in the fridge for up to 1 week.

5. SALT AND PEPPER SEASONING

6. SEASONED SOY SAUCE

7. SHRIMP CHILI OIL

8. XO SAUCE

5. SALT AND PEPPER SEASONING

MAKES 1¾ CUPS

2½ tablespoons kosher salt

1 tablespoon black peppercorns

1 tablespoon white peppercorns

1 tablespoon Szechuan peppercorns

1 cup store-bought fried garlic

1 tablespoon MSG

1 tablespoon sugar

Despite the name, this seasoning is more than just salt and pepper stirred together. It's a whole style of cooking. Cantonese people "salt and pepper" almost everything: pork chops, squid, chicken, shrimp, vegetables—you name it. A classic salt and pepper dish is whipped up in a wok, with the pork chop or squid, for example, tossed with the seasoning blend along with garlic, onions, and chilies. There's no set-in-stone ratio of salt and pepper, so everyone's seasoning will be a little different, but there will always be salt and there will always be white pepper. I mix in black peppercorns for extra heat, Szechuan peppercorns for that tingly craveability, and fried garlic to bring in a sweet garlicky punch that you cannot achieve with granulated garlic. Use the seasoning in Salt and Pepper Pork Schnitzel with Chinese Ranch (page 186) or Stovetop Salt and Pepper Popcorn (page 78).

1. In a small sauté pan over medium heat, toast the salt and black, white, and Szechuan peppercorns together, tossing often, until just fragrant, about 4 minutes. Pour the spice mix onto a small plate to cool quickly.

2. In a small blender (or coffee or spice grinder), combine the cooled spices, fried garlic, MSG, and sugar and grind to a fine, dusty powder. Store in an airtight container in your pantry with all your other spices for up to 1 month.

6.

SEASONED SOY SAUCE

MAKES 2 CUPS

1 cup dark soy sauce

1 cup Cantonese Chicken Broth (page 29) or water

½ cup sugar

¼ cup light soy sauce

1 (1-inch) piece ginger, sliced into 5 even pieces

1 scallion, cut crosswise into thirds

3 garlic cloves, smashed

1 star anise

1 bay leaf

1 small cinnamon stick

½ tablespoon MSG

¼ teaspoon fennel seeds

Light and dark soy sauces straight from the bottle can be overwhelmingly salty and overpowering. I would rarely use either as a dipping sauce or a finishing sauce. Instead, I like to infuse soy sauce with aromatics and spices while also reducing the salt level with unseasoned broth. The result, which is way more flavorful and way less salty, is the best kind of upgrade for any bottle of soy. Drizzle it over steamed fish (page 218).

1. In a medium pot, combine the dark soy sauce, broth, sugar, light soy sauce, ginger, scallion, garlic, star anise, bay leaf, cinnamon stick, MSG, and fennel seeds and bring to a boil over high heat.

2. Once the mixture is boiling, reduce the heat to medium-low and simmer for 15 minutes to allow the aromatics to infuse the liquid.

3. Pass the seasoned sauce through a fine-mesh strainer and discard the solids, then let cool completely. Store in an airtight container in the fridge for up to 2 weeks.

7. SHRIMP CHILI OIL

MAKES 4 CUPS

⅓ cup dried shrimp

2 cups dried Tianjin chilies (see Note)

1 cup store-bought fried shallots

1 tablespoon Szechuan peppercorns

5 star anise

1 tablespoon gochugaru (Korean chili flakes)

2 tablespoons toasted white sesame seeds

1 tablespoon kosher salt

2 teaspoons sugar

2 teaspoons MSG

3 cups neutral oil, preferably grapeseed

¼ cup fermented black soybeans, minced

1 tablespoon tomato paste

Although chili oil isn't super common in Cantonese cooking, there does happen to be a wide range of styles on the market, and you'll often find a jar or two in the fridge of most Cantonese households. If I'm buying, I lean toward the jars filled with an eyeballed ratio of roughly 75 percent crunchy, spicy, tasty bits and 25 percent oil. Those tend to be the most flavorful. But if I'm making chili oil at home, I like to toss in dried seafood for extra umami and *gochugaru* (Korean red chili flakes) for a light floral flavor and bright red color. My chili oil isn't the type that will make your tongue tingle from a spicy heat. Rather, it's the type that leaves your food with a newfound savory quality.

Note
Tianjin chilies are hot Chinese red chilies that aren't typically used in Cantonese cooking. They're much more popular in spicier northern Chinese dishes. Easy to source online and extremely shelf-stable, these chilies impart a sharp, fruity, vibrant flavor to this chili oil that is hard to replicate with any other variety.

1. In a small bowl, cover the dried shrimp with just enough warm water to submerge and soak for 15 minutes. Drain the shrimp and finely dice them. Set aside.

2. In a blender, combine the chilies, shallots, Szechuan peppercorns, star anise, and gochugaru and grind to a coarse powder.

3. In a medium heatproof bowl, whisk together the ground chili mixture, sesame seeds, salt, sugar, and MSG. Set aside.

4. Starting in a cold large pot or Dutch oven over medium heat, heat the oil with the soybeans, tomato paste, and rehydrated shrimp. Gently infuse the oil for 10 minutes, slowly and constantly stirring with a rubber spatula to ensure nothing burns.

5. After 10 minutes, raise the heat to high, bring the oil temperature up to about 300°F to 325°F, and then immediately remove the pot from the heat and pour the contents over the dried spice mixture. Chili oil can quickly go from toasty to burnt if you don't monitor the heat closely. If the oil is too cold, there's no depth of flavor. If it is too hot, it will taste scorched. I've found the most flavorful infusions happen in that sweet-spot range. Stir well to combine and then let cool completely. Store in an airtight container in the fridge for up to 1 month.

8.

XO SAUCE

MAKES 2¾ CUPS

¾ cup dried scallops

⅓ cup dried shrimp

⅓ cup dried anchovies

3 slices thick-cut bacon, cut into small dice

2 tablespoons water

1 small shallot, minced

8 garlic cloves, minced

1 (2-inch) piece ginger, minced

3 tablespoons Shaoxing wine

1 tablespoon toasted white sesame seeds

1 tablespoon gochugaru (Korean chili flakes)

1 tablespoon toasted sesame oil

1 tablespoon light soy sauce

2 teaspoons fennel seeds

1½ teaspoons sugar

1½ teaspoons MSG

1½ teaspoons fish sauce

2 cups neutral oil, preferably grapeseed

Developed in the 1980s by a chef in Hong Kong, this sauce leans on a trio of umami-heavy ingredients: dried scallops, dried shrimp, and cured Chinese pork (specifically, Jinhua ham), for their powerful flavors. I have never had a bad XO. This is an expensive sauce, as dried seafood does not come cheaply, but homemade beats store-bought any day because you can control the quality of the ingredients and the care that goes into the preparation. I use smoky bacon in this recipe because I can't get my hands on Jinhua ham. Unfortunately, the product is prohibited from importation into the United States, and regular Chinese cured bacon is too sweet for this sauce. Fun fact about the recipe's name: Although the sauce contains no alcohol, it was dubbed XO sauce thanks to Cantonese people's deep love of Cognac, specifically Hennessy X.O, an aged and expensive spirit. In Hong Kong, the term *XO* is often used to signify a product that is extra luxurious.

1. In a medium pot, bring a steamer setup (see page 43) to a rapid simmer over medium-high heat. Add the scallops, shrimp, and anchovies to a small steaming tray. Carefully lower the steaming tray onto the steaming rack. Cover and steam the dried seafood until soft, 10 to 15 minutes. Once the seafood has softened, remove the tray from the steamer setup and set the seafood aside to cool.

2. Add the cooled seafood to a food processor and pulse until the scallops are shredded into skinny strands and the shrimp and anchovies look like they have been coarsely chopped. Set the seafood aside.

3. In a small pot over low heat, combine the bacon and water and cook, stirring occasionally, until the bacon renders most of its fat and begins to brown and crisp up along the edges and the water has evaporated, about 10 minutes. Raise the heat to medium-high, add the shallot, garlic, and ginger, and sweat them in the oil, stirring often to prevent any browning, until fragrant and soft, about 5 minutes. Add the reserved seafood, wine, sesame seeds, gochugaru, sesame oil, soy sauce, fennel seeds, sugar, MSG, and fish sauce and stir with a spoon until well mixed, scraping to prevent sticking.

4. Reduce the heat to low and pour in the grapeseed oil. Bring the oil to a simmer and cook, stirring every so often, until the sauce is fragrant and infused, about 5 minutes. Remove from the heat and let cool completely. Store in an airtight container in the fridge for up to 2 weeks.

EQUIPMENT LIST

I've always said a cluttered space means a cluttered mind.

That philosophy strongly applies to my kitchen drawers and cabinets. I don't love single-use gadgets, and I don't own any specialty equipment. A lot can be done with the basics that you probably already own. That's why this book was developed with the mindset that you shouldn't have to go out and purchase any new, shiny pieces of equipment. Your baking sheets, mixing bowls, pots, and pans should be enough to tackle just about everything. But if you happen to be in the market for something new (and have the space), here are the few things I'd recommend you slowly add to your collection.

CANDY / DEEP-FRY THERMOMETER

Half the battle when frying at home is monitoring the oil temperature. If your oil is too hot, you run the risk of burning your shrimp sticks (page 88). If it's too cold, your Stuffed Golden Lava French Toast with Salted Duck Egg Custard (page 66) will soak up all the frying oil and turn soggy. A candy thermometer takes a lot of the guesswork out of frying. Look for one that gently clips on to the edge of your pot to keep your hands free to work and clear of the hot oil.

CAST-IRON AND CARBON-STEEL SKILLETS

These heavy-bottomed pans are amazing at getting really hot, retaining that heat, and cooking your food super evenly. Cast iron is definitely heavier to handle than carbon steel, but both can be nonstick if you take the time to clean, dry, and season properly after each and every use. A 12-inch skillet is perfect for just about any recipe in this book and for pretty much any recipe in any other book too.

CLEAVER
(and a Heavy-Duty Rubber Cutting Board)

A cleaver, like any sharp knife, is great for slicing, dicing, and chopping. But unlike a traditional chef's knife, it's extremely hefty with a sturdy handle, perfect for butchering a lobster or breaking down a chicken with ease. I like a carbon-steel cleaver. It's sharper, which means you have more control over the blade, and it stays that way longer than your average stainless-steel knife. Carbon steel can rust if you don't take care of it, much like your cast-iron and carbon-steel skillets. Use a thick rubber cutting board for chopping to avoid damaging your countertop, and if you don't plan to use the cleaver for a while, rub a bit of neutral oil over the blade after cleaning and thoroughly drying it. I prefer a rubber cutting board because the material is flexible, which means it won't warp, and rubber won't dull or damage your knife as quickly as wood or plastic.

DIGITAL SCALE

I don't always use a scale, but it's great for precise baking measurements. Your ½ cup flour may be a little bigger than my ½ cup flour, and it probably won't be the end of the world. But if you have the scale, we can have practically the same results for our Milk Bread Buns (page 60) and Toasted Sesame Shortbread (page 244).

FINE-MESH STRAINER AND NUT MILK BAG

Used together or separately, these tools are great for straining creamy Soy Milk (page 70), creamier Iced Black Sesame Milk (page 73), and Cantonese Chicken Broth (page 29). A fine-mesh strainer also comes in handy when rinsing rice, ensuring the ideal water-to-rice ratio for perfectly fluffy cooked grains.

PLASTIC WRAP

Buy the big restaurant-grade box. It will last your whole life, and it won't drive you mad with the flimsy box and the cheap-quality plastic that barely sticks.

STAINLESS-STEEL STEAMING TRAY
(and a Steaming Rack)

If you happen to be in an Asian grocery store, swing by the kitchen-equipment aisle and snag a few stainless-steel steaming trays for a couple of bucks each. They're great for steaming, for setting up a dredging station, for baking, or even for serving dinner. If you plan on steaming, you'll also need a steaming rack to elevate the tray above the water for the most even, gentle cooking. You can buy those at the grocery store, too. And if you're nervous about sticking your hands into a steamer to lift the tray out with just a kitchen towel, pick up a pair of plate-grabbing tongs at the store.

WOK
(and a Wok Ring)

I typically stay away from a wok in a home kitchen. You won't get that really high, high heat a restaurant wok burner produces, and honestly, it's kind of annoying that you can't stack a wok with your regular pots and pans. I do make an exception for a few dishes, however, such as Wok-Fried Egg (page 50) or a basic stir-fry. Woks can be great for frying long *Yauh Ja Gwai* (page 98), steaming extra-large dishes that don't fit in a regular pot, or stir-frying lots of food superfast. If you do decide to get a wok, make sure to get a carbon-steel one along with a wok ring that will allow it to sit snugly on your stovetop with no risk of it tipping over.

HOW TO SET UP A STEAMER

Steaming has a reputation for producing bland, boring diet food in a lot of American households, but in Chinese households, it's a gentle cooking technique to bring together a delicious dinner in one pot. Most people think steaming requires a colander or a steaming basket or even a bamboo steamer. But really all you need to set up a basic steamer is a large pot fitted with a secure lid, a steaming tray set on a steaming rack, and water. You don't need to buy anything special if you don't want to. That "tray" can be a flat-bottomed plate with a one-inch lip (think pie plate or cake pan or even a shallow bowl) in almost all the recipes that call for a metal steaming tray in this book. You can make a "rack" from a small, flat-bottomed bowl placed upside down on the bottom of the pot. The goal is simply to lift the steaming tray out of the boiling water, allowing the steam to rise. You can even sub in a large bowl for the "lid" if you need to add more height to the pot. The end goal with this method is to create a tightly sealed environment within the pot to trap the steam evaporating off the boiling water. That trapped steam will slowly and gently cook your food.

Before you start steaming, keep in mind that steam temperatures run hotter than boiling water, so you need to be extra, extra cautious around the vapor. When the timer goes off on your Sizzling Steamed Fish with Seasoned Soy Sauce (page 218) or steamed egg custard (page 122), kill the heat, stand back when lifting the lid, and then use plate grabbers, tongs, or a dry, thick kitchen towel to pull the steaming tray from the hot pot.

1. SELECT A POT AND STEAMING TRAY: Your pot should be wider than your steaming tray by an inch or more. If the two are too close in size, the steam will struggle to rise along the edge of the pot. If a recipe calls for a large steamer setup, select a 12-inch (or wider) pot or large wok. If a recipe calls for a medium steamer setup, select a 10-inch (or wider) pot.

2. SELECT A STEAMING RACK: You want your steaming tray to be elevated right above—never touching—the simmering water.

3. FILL YOUR POT WITH WATER: You'll typically need only 2 or 3 inches of water for a quick steam, but you can easily check on the level when cooking and top off with boiling water as needed to ensure it never fully evaporates. Just make sure the water sits about ½ inch below the steaming tray.

4. HEAT YOUR STEAMER: With the lid on, turn the heat to high to bring the water to a boil quickly, then adjust the temperature per the recipes instructions. Now you're ready to steam. Keep the lid on to maintain that moist-heat cooking environment. For longer steaming times, check your water level occasionally and top off with boiling water as needed.

HOW TO BECOME THE MOST EFFICIENT HOME COOK

(From a Restaurant Cook)

Proper Preparation Prevents Poor Performance.

Fail to Prepare, Prepare to Fail.

These are mottoes I live by and ingrain in my cooks' brains at my restaurant. It's not hard to be a good cook, but it's very easy to be a sloppy one. All the recipes in this book were developed in a home kitchen with less than two feet of counter space, oftentimes with a tiny child functioning as a self-appointed project manager, tasting every bite as soon as his first tiny tooth popped through. It was important to us that everything in this cookbook was achievable in our home, because if we could manage with our limited space, it should be doable for all cooks, no matter their setup, as long as they work efficiently. So here are my tips for becoming the most efficient cook you can possibly be.

CLEAN YOUR SINK AND EMPTY YOUR DISHWASHER

There is nothing worse than spending the afternoon cooking before realizing your sink is filled to the brim with dirty dishes or your dishwasher is packed full of perfectly clean plates that need to be put away. Dishes pile up on the counter, on the table, in the sink. It can be overwhelming. Clear the sink of any cutlery and empty the dishwasher (if you have one) so you can load in dirty dishes as you work. Your workspace will stay clean and organized, and cleaning up after you eat will be a breeze.

SET UP A GARBAGE STATION

I learned this one from my years of watching *30-Minute Meals* with Rachael Ray as a kid. I never like to work directly into the trash bin, so when I'm prepping, I pop a big bowl on the countertop to dump in onion skins and ginger peels, eggshells and shallot roots, and other bits and bobs in order to keep my cutting board clear. I also want to work efficiently, and this bowl means no running from the trash to the workspace and back again. Just one swift dump of the bowl at the end of prep and that's it. No need to awkwardly bend over the trash can or compost bin while you work. Easy peasy.

SLAP ON A PAIR OF GLOVES

I have a massive box of latex gloves in two sizes stashed in the kitchen cabinet. If I'm working with raw meat or anything super greasy and messy, I reach for a pair of gloves. They help keep my fingers clean and clear of cross contamination without constantly needing to run over to the sink to wash and rewash my hands, making quick work of arduous tasks. Your hands are your best tools, after all.

SECURE YOUR CUTTING BOARD

Have you ever tried to slice an onion on a cutting board that skitters around the countertop as you cut? It's twice as difficult and unnecessarily dangerous. To prevent slippage, dampen a kitchen towel or paper towel and slip it underneath the board to secure it to the counter. If you're using the board to slice anything that may be juicy, such as cooked meats or ripe fruit, slide the cutting board into a baking sheet, creating a raised lip along the edge of the board to catch anything that drips. Everything will stay contained in one area, saving you from a big mess on your counter. Just make sure to slide that damp towel under the baking sheet to secure the whole setup.

LABEL. EVERYTHING.

A Sharpie and masking tape are your new best friends in the kitchen. I label everything religiously in my home and at work. That way, I know what I have and when it was prepared. This ensures my fridge, freezer, and dry storage stay nice and organized, and when I reach for a reserved sauce or broth, I know exactly when it was made. This is especially important for anything you're popping into the freezer, as it can be especially hard to tell what something is once it's frozen.

1
BREAKFAST

As a kid, I was never that into the classic American breakfast foods. Pancakes were too soggy, oatmeal was too gloopy, cereal with milk was too mushy. It wasn't until I visited Hong Kong for the very first time and sat down in a booth at an old-school *cha chaan teng*, the standard Hong Kong–style diner or café, that I realized what breakfast could really be. These diners, which emerged in the 1950s cooking affordable British-influenced dishes, serve up plates of delicate, fluffy scrambled eggs (page 53) with thick slices of milk toast slathered in sweetened condensed milk and deep-fried stuffed French toast oozing with peanut butter or salted duck egg custard (page 66), all flowing nonstop from a tiny kitchen. Cups of *yuen yeung* (page 74) and soy milk (page 70) and milk tea (page 74) are scattered across every table in sight. Breakfast should be this fun all the time. It needs to be. It is the most important meal of the day, after all.

Wok-Fried Egg	50
Hong Kong Egg Scramble	53
Nam Yu Maple Candied Bacon	54
Taro Root Diner Hash Browns with Sweet-and-Spicy Ketchup	57
Malted Chocolate Waffles	58
Milk Bread Buns with Butter	60
Steamed Then Fried Egg Sandwich	64
Stuffed Golden Lava French Toast with Salted Duck Egg Custard	66
Soy Milk	70
Iced Black Sesame Milk	73
Milk Tea	74
And a Bonus Recipe for Yuen Yeung (Coffee Milk Tea)	74

WOK-FRIED EGG

SERVES 4

I'm not a big proponent of using a wok in a home kitchen. You can often produce a satisfactory result for most dishes with a carbon-steel or cast-iron skillet on a high flame without adding an extra chunky piece of equipment to your collection. But my one big, glaring exception is this fried egg. The rounded bottom of the wok perfectly nestles an egg during a quick fry. The second a freshly cracked egg hits oil in a ripping-hot wok, the whites begin to crisp up and bubble, creating delicate lacy edges. And the beauty of this egg is that you barely touch it, and you definitely don't have to flip it. Just baste the top with oil to finish off the fry and you're done—you'll have the quickest fried egg with an almost set but still runny yolk.

½ cup neutral oil, preferably grapeseed

4 large eggs

Kosher salt and freshly ground white pepper

MSG

Oyster sauce or XO Sauce (page 37), to serve (optional)

1. Line a large plate with paper towels and set it near the stove. Heat a wok over high heat. Once you start to see the first wisps of smoke from the wok, swirl in the oil to coat the bottom and up the sides.

2. Working with one egg at a time, crack each into a small bowl. (I prefer to crack my eggs into a bowl rather than directly into the wok, in case the yolk breaks or there are loose bits of shell.) When the oil starts to shimmer, add the egg and immediately season to taste with salt, pepper, and MSG.

3. Using a large spoon, baste the egg with the hot oil until the whites crisp along the edges and puff up in the center, almost fully covering the yolk, about 1 minute. When the edges reach your desired crispness, use a slotted spatula or spoon to transfer the egg to the paper towel–lined plate to drain off any excess oil.

4. Repeat with the remaining eggs. Transfer the eggs to individual plates, drizzle with oyster sauce (if using), and serve immediately.

HONG KONG EGG SCRAMBLE

SERVES 1

My first taste of Hong Kong scrambled eggs was at a booth in a random *cha chaan teng* in 2016. The eggs were soft and pillowy, custardy and light. They were unlike any other scrambled eggs I had experienced before. I soon learned there were a few tricks to making this style scramble. Ingredients like evaporated milk and cornstarch are key, as is making sure everything is whisked together really well. The evaporated milk adds a nice bit of fat that gives the eggs a silkier texture. The starch is mixed with water to make a slurry, a common technique in Chinese cooking to create thicker, more luscious sauces and impossibly fluffy eggs that won't deflate. For a *cha chaan teng* experience at home, serve the scramble alongside a cup of hot Milk Tea (page 74) to wash it all down.

Tip
Turn these eggs into a sandwich. Layer your fluffy eggs on a fresh milk bread bun (page 60) with a few slices of thinly sliced ham, Spam, or Nam Yu Maple Candied Bacon (page 54) and American cheese.

2 tablespoons evaporated milk

2 tablespoons water

1 teaspoon cornstarch

1 teaspoon neutral oil, preferably grapeseed

3 large eggs

¼ teaspoon kosher salt

⅛ teaspoon MSG

⅛ teaspoon freshly ground white pepper

1 tablespoon unsalted butter

1. In a small bowl, whisk together the evaporated milk, water, cornstarch, and oil until the cornstarch is fully dissolved.

2. Crack the eggs into the bowl and add the salt, MSG, and pepper. Whisk until the mixture is completely homogenous with no streaky bits.

3. Heat a small nonstick skillet over medium-high heat. Add the butter and swirl it around the bottom and up the sides of the pan until completely melted and foamy.

4. When the foaming has subsided, gently pour in the egg mixture. Using a rubber spatula, and working around the pan in a clockwise motion, quickly and continuously push the egg mixture toward the center until soft peaks form in the curds but the eggs are still a little runny, about 1 minute. The eggs will continue to cook slightly once they are removed from the pan, so you don't want to cook them all the way. Serve immediately (or see Tip).

NAM YU MAPLE CANDIED BACON

SERVES 4

The inspiration for this candied bacon came from the little prepackaged bags of chicken biscuits my mom used to buy from random bakeries for a midday shopping snack. Contrary to the name, chicken biscuits are not made with any sort of chicken product. Rather, the thin, crunchy, candy-like cookies are studded with big chunks of pork fat and swirls of *nam yu*. Almost cheesy, *nam yu* is fermented red bean curd with a nicely balanced sweet-and-savory flavor straight out of the jar. Sometimes labeled as red bean curd or wet bean curd, these soft red cubes have briny, umami undertones similar to *fuyu* (page 18) but a totally different flavor. Think sweet, savory, umami. Those chicken biscuits highlight how *nam yu* perfectly complements fatty pork products in sweet treats, and when whisked into maple syrup, it becomes a savory, sweet, sticky glaze to brush over thick slabs of bacon.

1. Preheat the oven to 400°F. Line a baking sheet with parchment paper (for easy cleanup) and fit a wire rack large enough to hold the bacon in a single layer on top.

2. In a small bowl, whisk together the maple syrup and nam yu cubes and liquid until the curds dissolve, forming a smooth glaze.

3. Lay the bacon slices flat on the wire rack in a single layer spaced evenly. Generously brush the top of each slice with the glaze.

4. Bake for 15 minutes. Then rotate the baking sheet back to front and continue to bake until the bacon is cooked to your preferred crispness, up to 10 minutes longer. I personally like thick-cut bacon that still has a bite and chew to it. Let the bacon cool on the baking sheet for 10 minutes to allow the glaze to set up a bit before serving.

¼ cup pure maple syrup

2 tablespoons nam yu (fermented red bean curd), cubes and liquid (I like Golden Crop brand)

1 pound thick-cut bacon

TARO ROOT DINER HASH BROWNS
with Sweet-and-Spicy Ketchup

SERVES 5

I love potatoes. Boiled potatoes, fried potatoes, mashed potatoes. But the most perfect potato form is an extra-crispy, golden brown hash brown hot off an extremely well-seasoned diner flattop. I also happen to love taro, a nutty, earthy root vegetable that's great chunked up in hearty, homey braises and stews or fried into puffs to be wheeled around at dim sum halls. But you can also boil it, fry it, or mash it just like you would a potato. Most importantly, you can shred taro on a box grater, toss it with strands of frozen taters, and griddle it in clarified butter for a nuttier, sweeter take on classic diner-style hash browns. Devour them piping hot slathered with sweet-and-spicy ketchup, dunked in maple syrup, or as is with a generous hit of salt.

Note
Clarified butter is the key to achieving an even golden brown crust. Regular melted butter has milk solids that will burn before the hash browns have a chance to crisp up. You can buy ghee, or you can clarify your own butter by gently melting ½ pound unsalted butter over medium heat, skimming the milk solids off the top with a slotted spoon, and then using only the clear yellow butterfat.

1. PREPARE THE SWEET-AND-SPICY KETCHUP: In a small bowl, whisk together the ketchup, mirin, sriracha, and water, mixing well. Set aside.

2. PREPARE THE HASH BROWNS: Peel the taro root, then, using a food processor fitted with the grating blade or the large holes on a box grater, coarsely shred the taro into long strands to measure 2 cups. In a medium bowl, combine the taro, frozen hash browns, salt, MSG, and pepper and mix well. Using a rubber spatula, roughly divide the mixture into five portions in the bowl.

3. Top a baking sheet with a large wire rack and set it near the stove. In a large cast-iron skillet over medium heat, melt 2 to 3 tablespoons of the clarified butter (enough to coat the bottom of the pan). Working in batches to avoid crowding, add portions of the taro mixture to the pan and, using the back of a metal spatula, flatten each portion until it is ¼ inch thick. Slowly fry the hash browns, flipping once, until the center is cooked through and the exterior crisps up and turns golden brown, about 3 minutes per side. Using the spatula, transfer the hash browns to the wire rack. Repeat with the remaining taro mixture, adding more clarified butter to the pan for each batch. Serve with big dollops (or a smiley face squeeze) of the sweet-and-spicy ketchup.

SWEET-AND-SPICY KETCHUP
½ cup ketchup

¼ cup mirin (Japanese cooking wine)

2 tablespoons sriracha

2 tablespoons water

HASH BROWNS
1 small taro root, about ½ pound

2 cups frozen shredded hash browns (no need to thaw)

1 tablespoon kosher salt

1 teaspoon MSG

¼ teaspoon freshly ground white pepper

½ cup clarified butter (see Note) or ghee, divided

MALTED CHOCOLATE WAFFLES

MAKES 6 WAFFLES

Ovaltine is a Hong Kong staple by way of British colonization, a common theme with a lot of dishes you'll find on the menu at a *cha chaan teng*. The malted chocolate powder is perfectly delicious stirred into a glass of warm milk or sprinkled on a lightly toasted piece of milk bread with a drizzle of condensed milk and a pat of butter. But I like it best whisked into a chocolaty waffle batter that's cooked off until crispy and light. It's all the craveable parts of classic Ovaltine toast with double the chocolate and double the nooks and crannies for the puddles of melty butter and condensed milk to pool.

1. In a medium bowl, whisk together the flour, Ovaltine powder, cocoa powder, baking powder, salt, and baking soda.

2. In a separate medium bowl, whisk together the buttermilk, brown sugar, eggs, melted butter, and vanilla until there are no streaks of egg and the sugar is dissolved.

3. Fold the wet ingredients into the dry ingredients, taking care not to overmix. A few lumps are fine. Let the batter rest for 15 minutes.

4. Meanwhile, preheat a waffle iron according to the manufacturer's instructions. Using a pastry brush or paper towel, lightly brush the grids of the waffle iron with melted butter.

5. Spoon the batter into the iron; the amount of batter will vary depending on your waffle iron, but start with about ¼ cup and add more if necessary. Cook until the waffles are crispy and light and the smell of chocolate fills your kitchen; the timing will vary depending on your iron. Repeat with the remaining batter, brushing the iron with more melted butter between each waffle.

6. TO SERVE: Plate the waffles immediately and garnish with a drizzle of condensed milk, a dusting of Ovaltine powder, and big pats of butter. You can hold the waffles on a wire rack on a baking sheet in a 200°F oven until ready to garnish and eat, or you can cool them and toss them into the freezer for popping into the toaster to reheat for future breakfasts.

1⅓ cups (175g) all-purpose flour

1⅓ cups (150g) Ovaltine malted drink powder (I like European formula Ovaltine)

2 tablespoons (12g) unsweetened cocoa powder (natural or Dutch-processed)

1 teaspoon (4g) baking powder

1 teaspoon (3g) kosher salt

¼ teaspoon (1.5g) baking soda

1 cup (227g) buttermilk

⅓ cup (75g) packed dark brown sugar

2 large eggs, at room temperature

2½ tablespoons (35g) unsalted butter, melted and cooled, plus more melted butter for the waffle maker

1 teaspoon (4g) pure vanilla extract

TO SERVE

Sweetened condensed milk

Ovaltine malted drink powder

Unsalted butter

MILK BREAD BUNS
with Butter

MAKES 6 BUNS

Very few bites are better than a buttery brioche roll or a squishy potato bun, but a warm, fluffy milk bread bun is truly unbeatable. The key to this recipe is an Asian bread-making technique known as *tangzhong*, which yields the softest, squishiest bread. *Tangzhong* is a cooked and cooled paste of milk and flour that adds moisture to the dough from the jump, resulting in pillowy buns and loaves that won't stale immediately. Use these buns for your Steamed Then Fried Egg Sandwich (page 64) and FFLT (Fried Fish, Lettuce, Tomato) Sandwich (page 221), or simply slather the still-warm buns with butter and sprinkle with flaky salt.

1. PREPARE THE TANGZHONG: In a small pot over medium heat, using a rubber spatula, mix together the milk, flour, and water until the mixture thickens to the consistency of mashed potatoes. This should only take a minute or so, but make sure to stir continuously to prevent the mixture from scorching. Remove the pot from the heat and set aside to cool until the mixture is just warm to the touch.

2. PREPARE THE MILK BREAD: Measure the milk in a microwave-safe cup measure and heat in a microwave until just warm to the touch, 20 to 30 seconds. In the bowl of a stand mixer, whisk together the warm milk and yeast. Scrape the partially cooled tangzhong into the bowl and add the flour, sugar, egg, and kosher salt. Fit the mixer with the dough hook and mix on medium speed until the mixture begins to pull away from the sides of the bowl and forms a shaggy dough, 2 to 3 minutes.

3. Reduce the mixer speed to medium-low and toss in the butter cubes, one at a time, mixing until each cube is fully incorporated before adding the next one. This can take up to 10 minutes. Scrape down the sides of the bowl with a rubber spatula or bench scraper, then increase the mixer speed to medium and knead until the dough is soft and bouncy, about 5 minutes.

4. Grease a medium bowl with oil. Using a rubber spatula or a plastic bench scraper, transfer the dough from the mixer bowl to the greased bowl. Gently shape the dough into a rough ball. Cover the bowl with a large, lightly damp kitchen towel or with plastic wrap and let the dough proof on the counter at room temperature for 1 to 2 hours. The dough should double in size. If your kitchen is chilly, you can pop the dough into the oven and turn the light on. Just make sure not to turn the oven on.

TANGZHONG

¼ cup (56g) whole milk

2 tablespoons (20g) all-purpose flour

2 tablespoons (35g) water

MILK BREAD

½ cup (113g) whole milk

1 packet (2¼ teaspoons/7g) active dry yeast

2½ cups (300g) all-purpose flour

¼ cup (50g) sugar

1 large egg, at room temperature

1 teaspoon (3g) kosher salt

3 tablespoons (42g) unsalted butter, cubed and at room temperature

Neutral oil, preferably grapeseed, to grease

5. Line a baking sheet with parchment paper or a nonstick baking mat. Punch down the dough, then turn it out onto a clean work surface. Divide the dough into six even pieces. If you have a kitchen scale, each piece should weigh about 110 grams. Keep all the dough portions under the large kitchen towel or piece of plastic wrap so they don't dry out. Working with one piece at a time, cup your hand over the dough and drag it across the work surface, moving your hand in a circular motion as you do to form a tight ball. Place the ball on the prepared baking sheet and repeat with the remaining pieces, spacing the balls evenly apart on the pan.

6. Cover the balls loosely with the kitchen towel or piece of plastic wrap and let proof on the counter at room temperature for 40 to 45 minutes. The buns are ready to bake when they are puffed up but hold a small imprint when poked. While the buns proof, preheat the oven to 350°F.

7. PREPARE THE EGG WASH: In a small bowl, whisk together the egg and milk until there are no streaks of egg.

8. Brush the egg wash over the tops of the buns and then sprinkle evenly with the sesame seeds and flaky salt. Bake the buns until golden brown, 20 to 22 minutes. Remove from the oven and transfer to a wire rack to cool.

9. TO SERVE: Slice the buns open while they are still a little warm. Slather with butter and sprinkle with flaky salt.

EGG WASH AND TOPPINGS

1 large egg

1 tablespoon whole milk

2 tablespoons toasted white sesame seeds

1 tablespoon Maldon flaky salt

TO SERVE

Unsalted butter, at room temperature

Maldon flaky salt

BREAKFAST

STEAMED THEN FRIED EGG SANDWICH

MAKES 2 SANDWICHES

My first job in the food world was working behind the deli counter at my friend's family bodega. At fifteen, I was running that sandwich counter every day after school. We called ourselves the deli technicians, and we pumped out breakfast sandwiches all afternoon and into the night. Any combo you could think of, we made it. Baconeggandcheese saltpepperketchup at any hour of the day, no problem. This breakfast sandwich is an ode to that time behind that counter. I swapped out the classic scramble for a fluffy steamed egg that's lightly coated in panko and then fried like a piece of *katsu*. The bacon is replaced with Spam, a nod to *cha chaan teng*s, and the roll is now a pillowy sesame milk bread bun. But the cheese is still two slices of American, which will always be the perfect melty cheese for any breakfast sandwich.

1. Line the bottom and sides of an 8½ x 4½-inch loaf pan with plastic wrap, leaving a 2-inch overhang tucked tightly along the long sides. These flaps will be your handles to remove the steamed egg from the pan later on. Make sure the plastic wrap lies flat along the bottom and sides of the pan so the egg mixture will steam evenly.

2. PREPARE THE STEAMED EGG: In a large bowl, whisk together the eggs until homogenous. Whisk in the garlic chives, water, wine, salt, MSG, and pepper. Pour the egg custard mixture into the prepared loaf pan. Lay an additional long sheet of plastic wrap on the counter, then gently place the custard-filled loaf pan on one end of the plastic wrap. With the plastic wrap handles still tucked to the sides, bring the remaining plastic wrap over the top of the pan to meet the bottom in one continuous tight sheet. Wrap as tightly as possible without touching the egg mixture to avoid any excess moisture getting in.

3. In a large pot, bring a steamer setup (see page 43) to a rapid simmer over medium-high heat. Carefully lower the loaf pan onto the steaming rack. Cover and steam the egg for 15 minutes. Be patient and wait the full 15 minutes before lifting the lid to check on it. You're looking for the top of the custard to be smooth and uniform, with a tiny jiggle under the surface. Remove the loaf pan from the steamer setup and allow it to rest for 1 minute before removing the tightly wrapped plastic wrap from around the pan.

4. Let the steamed egg cool completely in the steaming tray. Then, using the plastic wrap handles, lift out the steamed egg and cut in half crosswise into two squares.

STEAMED EGG

6 large eggs

2 tablespoons thinly sliced flat green garlic chives or scallions (green tops only)

1½ tablespoons water

1½ teaspoons Shaoxing wine

1½ teaspoons kosher salt

½ teaspoon MSG

⅛ teaspoon freshly ground white pepper

5. FRY THE STEAMED EGG: Pour oil to a depth of at least 2 inches (or halfway up the sides, whichever is shallower) of a medium pot or Dutch oven and heat over medium-high heat to 350°F. Line a plate with paper towels and set it near the stove.

6. While the oil heats, set up the dredging station. Put the cornstarch into a wide, shallow dish, the beaten egg into another shallow dish, and the panko into a third shallow dish. One at a time, dust the steamed egg squares with the cornstarch, gently shaking off the excess; then dip into the egg, letting the excess drip off; and finally, coat with the panko. Lay the breaded pieces on a baking sheet until ready to fry.

7. Gently lower one breaded egg square into the oil and deep-fry, flipping halfway through, until golden brown on all sides, about 2 minutes. Using a slotted spoon or spider, transfer to the paper towel–lined plate to drain. Repeat with the remaining egg square.

8. In the same pot, deep-fry the Spam (working in two batches if needed) until it takes on a little bit of color, about 1 minute, then transfer to the same paper towel–lined plate.

9. TO SERVE: Toast your bun of choice and slather the top half of each bun with ketchup. Layer a fried egg square on each bun bottom and top with one slice of cheese and one slice of Spam per sandwich. Close with the bun tops and serve at once.

TO FRY

Neutral oil, preferably grapeseed

¼ cup cornstarch

1 large egg, beaten

½ cup panko breadcrumbs

2 (¼-inch-thick) slices low-sodium Spam

TO SERVE

2 milk bread buns (page 60), potato buns, brioche buns, or Hawaiian buns, split

Ketchup

2 slices American cheese

STUFFED GOLDEN LAVA FRENCH TOAST
with Salted Duck Egg Custard

SERVES 6

Hong Kong French toast is not your typical singular slice of stale bread dunked in a milky egg mixture before a gentle cook in a pat of butter. It's three stacks of crustless, plush milk bread layered with thick smears of peanut butter and Ovaltine, battered, deep-fried, and then doused in sweetened condensed milk. And sometimes, the center of the middle layer is hollowed out and stuffed with salted duck egg yolk custard that turns oozy and molten in the fryer—impossibly luscious and rich, buttery, and, of course, salty too.

Note

There are two types of salted duck eggs on the market. Whole salted eggs in plastic cartons and cured salted duck egg yolks. You want the latter for this recipe. The beautiful jewel-like, bright-orange yolks are sold in vacuum-sealed bags online and in the refrigerated aisle of Chinese supermarkets. Freeze any leftover yolks in an airtight container for future French toast needs.

1. Line the bottom of an 8-inch square baking dish with parchment paper.

2. PREPARE THE SALTED DUCK EGG CUSTARD: In a medium pot, bring a steamer setup (see page 43) to a rapid simmer over medium-high heat. Add the egg yolks to a small steaming tray, then carefully lower the steaming tray onto the steaming rack. Cover and steam the egg yolks until soft, about 12 minutes. Remove the tray from the steamer setup and set the egg yolks aside to cool.

3. Remove the steamer rack from the pot and discard the water. Wipe the pot dry, then place over medium heat. Pour in the water and whisk in the gelatin until completely dissolved, about 1 minute, then immediately remove from the heat.

4. In a small blender or mini food processor, combine the dissolved gelatin water, cooled egg yolks, and coconut milk and process until smooth. Pour the yolk mixture back into the medium pot and whisk in the sugar, condensed milk, malt powder, custard powder, and cornstarch until all the dry ingredients have dissolved and the mixture is smooth. Set over medium heat and cook, whisking constantly, until slightly thickened, about 3 to 4 minutes.

SALTED DUCK EGG CUSTARD

5 salted duck egg yolks (see Note)

½ cup water

1 teaspoon powdered gelatin

¼ cup unsweetened coconut milk (I like Chaokoh brand)

3 tablespoons sugar

3 tablespoons sweetened condensed milk

2 tablespoons malt powder

1 tablespoon custard powder (I like Lion brand)

2 teaspoons cornstarch

3½ tablespoons unsalted butter, cubed

RECIPE AND INGREDIENTS CONTINUE

5. Remove the pot from the stovetop and toss in the butter cubes, one at a time, whisking after each addition until incorporated and then whisking until fully emulsified and smooth. This mixture will continue to thicken off the heat. Pass the custard through a fine-mesh strainer into the prepared baking dish, then cover and freeze until solid, 3 to 4 hours.

6. Once the custard is frozen, invert the baking pan onto a cutting board then peel off the parchment and cut into six uniform rectangles, each roughly 4 by 2½ inches.

7. ASSEMBLE THE FRENCH TOAST: Use three slices of bread per custard block. Place the custard block on top of one piece of bread to use as a guide to cut a window that will fit the block snugly inside the slice. The window should be at least ¾ inch wider than the custard block, so if the custard is too large for the bread slice, trim the edges of the custard and stack the excess on top of the block before sandwiching. This will become the middle piece of the French toast. Take the remaining two slices and spread a thin layer of condensed milk along the outer edges of each slice. This will act as the glue to hold the slices together. Lay the bottom bread slice milk side up. Top with the middle slice with the custard block and then finish with the third slice, milk side down. Using your fingers, gently press the edges of the assembled French toast together. Then cut the crusts off with a serrated knife. Repeat with the remaining bread slices and custard blocks.

8. FRY THE FRENCH TOAST: Pour oil to a depth of at least 3 inches (or halfway up the sides, whichever is shallower) of a large pot or Dutch oven and heat over medium-high heat to 350°F. Line a large plate with paper towels and set it near the stove.

9. Crack the eggs into a wide, shallow baking dish. Whisk until homogenous. One at a time, dunk each assembled French toast into the eggs, coating it well on all six sides to ensure the slices are properly sealed together. Lay the breaded French toast on a baking sheet until ready to fry.

10. Working one at a time, using your hands, gently lower the French toast into the oil away from your body to prevent oil splatter, and deep-fry, flipping halfway through, until golden brown on all sides, about 2 minutes. Transfer to the paper towel–lined plate to drain. Pat off any excess oil. Repeat with the remaining French toasts.

11. TO SERVE: Top each French toast with a big pat of butter, a drizzle of condensed milk, and pinch of flaky salt.

FRENCH TOAST

18 slices milk bread or white sandwich bread, each about 4 inches square and ½ inch thick

Sweetened condensed milk, for spreading

Neutral oil, preferably grapeseed, for frying

8 large eggs

TO SERVE

Unsalted butter

Sweetened condensed milk

Maldon flaky salt

BREAKFAST

SOY MILK

MAKES 6 TO 8 SERVINGS

I'm pretty convinced I'm allergic to soy milk. But one of my fondest memories is of the scent of sweetened soy milk perfuming the whole house as it simmered away on the stovetop for hours. I always asked my mom if I could help her make it on the weekends. She would have me hop up onto a chair next to her so she could supervise. At the time, I was too young to run the operation on my own and too short to use the immersion blender to blend the soybeans we had soaked overnight. That first taste was always the sweetest, the nuttiest. Even now, I'll always sample a sip or two of fresh soy milk just to bring me back to that time. It's worth the tiny scratch in the back of my throat.

1. In a medium bowl, combine the soybeans with cold water to cover by about 2 inches. Cover and refrigerate for at least 8 hours or up to 12 hours.

2. Drain the soaked soybeans in a colander set in the sink, discarding the soaking liquid.

3. In a blender, combine half of the drained beans with 5 cups of the water and blend until creamy. Pour the blended mixture into a large pot. Repeat with the remaining beans and remaining 5 cups water, add to the pot, and stir to mix.

4. Set the pot over low heat, bring the mixture to a gentle simmer, and simmer for 3 hours. There's no need to stir. Just make sure the heat is low because the soy milk will scorch if the heat is too high. If any foam rises to the top, skim it off with a big spoon. After 3 hours, the soy milk should taste sweet and nutty, instead of vegetal like the soybeans.

5. When the soy milk is ready, line a fine-mesh strainer with a cold-brew strainer bag, nut milk bag, or cheesecloth. Set the strainer over a large pitcher or medium bowl. Remove the soy milk mixture from the heat and strain through the prepared strainer in two batches.

6. Whisk in the sugar (if using) to dissolve while the soy milk is still hot. Sweeten and serve warm or chilled. Soy milk will keep in an airtight container in the fridge for up to 5 days.

2 heaping cups dried soybeans

10 cups water, divided

¼ cup sugar (optional)

ICED BLACK SESAME MILK

SERVES 4

My mom never made black sesame soup from scratch, but whenever she had a craving, she loved the packets of powdered soup mix that you stir into a hot cup of water for an instant snack. It was sweet and nutty with just a hint of black sesame bitterness, but the texture was never quite my favorite because the glutinous rice in the mix gave the soup body and thickness that sometimes veered gloopy rather than creamy. I always wanted the soup to be more of a sipper—chuggable, if you will—more like soy milk but sweetened and lightly spiced like horchata. So I ditched the rice and served it over ice and now this is what I crave.

1. In a small sauté pan, toast the sesame seeds, cinnamon stick, and star anise over medium-high heat, tossing every so often to ensure the seeds and spices don't burn, until fragrant. The seeds should be warm to the touch but should not smoke. Reduce the heat if you begin to see wisps of smoke. Remove from the heat when toasted.

2. Pour 3 cups of the water into a small bowl, add the seeds and spices, and stir to ensure all the seeds are saturated. Cover and place in the fridge to soak for 8 to 12 hours.

3. Drain the seed mixture into a fine-mesh strainer, discarding all the soaking liquid. Transfer the seeds and spices to a blender, add the remaining 2 cups water, and blitz on high speed until the solids are finely ground, about 1½ minutes.

4. Line a fine-mesh strainer with a nut milk bag and place the strainer over a medium bowl. Pour the blended sesame mixture into the prepared strainer, then squeeze the nut milk bag to ensure you get every bit of toasty, nutty sesame flavor out. Discard the pulp.

5. Rinse the blender, then add the strained sesame mixture, evaporated milk, and condensed milk to it. Blend on high speed for 30 seconds to incorporate everything. Transfer to an airtight container and chill in the fridge for at least 30 minutes before serving. The sesame milk will keep for up to 3 days.

6. When ready to serve, give the black sesame milk a good shake, then pour over ice for an extra-refreshing sip.

1 cup black sesame seeds

1 small cinnamon stick

1 star anise

5 cups cold water, divided

1½ cups evaporated milk

5 tablespoons sweetened condensed milk

MILK TEA

MAKES 4 CUPS

A traditional, well-made cup of milk tea from a *cha chaan teng* is very different from the lukewarm cup of barely brewed Lipton with a splash of milk you'll find at any bakery in Chinatown. The former is an aggressively brewed and highly caffeinated drink swirled with sweetened condensed milk and evaporated milk to take the harsh tannic edge off. The milky combination makes the tea silky smooth, a little sweet, and very crushable, hot or iced.

1. In a small pot, bring the water to a boil with the lid on. Once it is boiling, sprinkle in the tea leaves. Reduce the heat to low and simmer for 15 minutes with the lid on.

2. Line a strainer with a coffee filter and place it over a pitcher. Strain the brewed tea through the prepared strainer.

3. Add the condensed milk and evaporated milk to the tea and whisk until fully incorporated. The color should be milky brown. Serve warm or over ice. The tea will keep in an airtight container in the fridge for up to 3 days.

4½ cups water

½ cup Lipton orange pekoe loose leaf tea

½ cup sweetened condensed milk

½ cup evaporated milk

AND A BONUS RECIPE FOR
Yuen Yeung (Coffee Milk Tea)

Milk tea's equally popular *cha chaan teng* counterpart is yuen yeung, a simple mixture of brewed black coffee and milk tea. I've always preferred *yuen yeung* that was more milk tea than coffee, but this is a totally customizable recipe, so you can play around with how much coffee you choose to add. To make it: In a mug or glass, stir together ¾ cup milk tea and ¼ cup brewed back coffee. Taste and adjust the sweetness to your liking with condensed milk and evaporated milk, if you'd like. Serve warm or over ice. for breakfast, or steaming hot over a scoop of vanilla ice cream for an after-dinner treat. It will keep in an airtight container in the fridge for up to 3 days. (Makes 1 cup)

2
SNACKS

Every evening after dinner, when everyone is fed and the kid is bathed and in bed and the apartment is cleaned and the emails have been answered, I sit in my bed and feast. Chips and dips, popcorn too. Crunchy things, slightly sweet things, savory things. Leftover fries, leftover wings, leftover leftovers. The night is not complete until I've had a full second dinner made up of snacks. Snacking was and always will be my favorite way to eat.

Stovetop Salt and Pepper Popcorn 78

Fish Mix 81

Jammy Marble Tea Eggs 82

Tinned Dace Dip 85

Lemon Cola Chicken Wings 86

Shrimp Sticks with
Ginger-Scallion Tartar Sauce 88

Shrimp Cocktail with Fuyu Chive Aioli
and Gingery Cocktail Sauce 90

Pork and Chive Dumplings with
Caramelized Onion Soy Butter 94

Piggies in Scallion Milk Bread Blankets 96

Yauh Ja Gwai (Fried Crullers) 98

STOVETOP SALT AND PEPPER POPCORN

SERVES 2

There are very few noises more satisfying than the pop, pop, pop of kernels bursting into light and airy pieces of popcorn. Maybe the sound of butter slowly melting and sputtering in a pot, or onions sizzling and frizzling in a pan? In any case, this specific popping-popcorn noise I'm talking about only truly happens on the stovetop. The microwave kind is perfectly fine in the case of a snacking emergency, but stovetop popcorn is significantly more delicious. And this particular stovetop popcorn is something special. It has a hint of Szechuan peppercorn that makes your mouth pucker up in the best way possible. It's so zippy and salty and peppery that it's next to impossible to share the bowl with anyone else. I'm typing up this headnote one-handed so I can keep shoveling whole fistfuls of the stuff into my mouth!

1. In a medium heavy pot or Dutch oven, heat the oil over medium-high heat. Once the oil is shimmering, add the popcorn kernels and cover the pot almost all the way with a lid, leaving a small crack open for steam to escape. Continuously shake the pot over the heat to pop every kernel and to avoid burning. Once you no longer hear those telltale pops (wait for at least 8 seconds before deciding the kernels are done popping), remove the pot from the heat and dump the popcorn into a large bowl.

2. Pick out any kernels that failed to pop. Pour in the butter and sprinkle the seasoning evenly over the popcorn. Toss to distribute the butter and seasoning evenly. Serve immediately.

2 tablespoons neutral oil, preferably grapeseed

¼ cup popcorn kernels

3 tablespoons unsalted butter, melted

4 teaspoons Salt and Pepper Seasoning (page 34)

FISH MIX

MAKES 6 TO 7 CUPS

There used to be an outpost of the Hong Kong snack food franchise Aji Ichiban on Mott Street in Chinatown just around the corner from my grandparents' place. It was one of those snacky candy shops where you bought everything by the pound—dried plums that made your mouth water, every flavor of fish jerky, gummy bears and cola candies, dehydrated cantaloupe that looked like little gems, candied squid, and baby crabs. Every bin was topped with a colored glass dish and a set of tiny tongs, practically begging shoppers to nibble on samples as they perused the aisle. I never thought too hard about what I scooped into my bag. I just knew to take a mix-and-match approach—a bit of salty, a bit of sweet, and a bit of savory. Delicious every time. Whenever I'm missing that shop (and feeling snackish), I whip up this crispy, sticky fish mix to fill the hole in my heart.

1. Preheat the oven to 275°F. Line a baking sheet with parchment paper or a nonstick baking mat.

2. PREPARE THE FISH MIX: In a large bowl, toss together the Corn Chex, rice cereal, peanuts, Fritos, Goldfish, dried anchovies, dried shrimp, and sesame seeds, mixing well. Set aside.

3. PREPARE THE SYRUP: In a small pot, combine the corn syrup, butter, brown sugar, honey, fish sauce, soy sauce, MSG, gochugaru, and garlic and stir to mix well. Place over high heat and bring to a boil. Boil for 2 minutes to form a loose syrup, stirring occasionally, then remove from the heat and pour over the fish mix. Using a rubber spatula, toss together to coat evenly.

4. Scatter the fish mix evenly over the prepared baking sheet. Bake for 45 to 50 minutes. At the 30-minute mark, pull the mix from the oven and give it a quick stir, then return the pan to the oven, rotating the pan back to front, and bake for the final 15 to 20 minutes. The mix is ready when it is a dark, even brown.

5. Let the mix cool on the pan for 30 minutes, then break up the pieces into evenish chunks. The mixture should be crispy in some bites, a little tacky in others, and very savory. Eat immediately, or store in an airtight container in the pantry for up to 1 week.

FISH MIX

1½ cups Corn Chex

1 cup puffed rice cereal

½ cup unsalted roasted peanuts

½ cup Fritos Original corn chips

¼ cup Goldfish crackers

¼ cup dried anchovies

¼ cup dried shrimp

¼ cup toasted white sesame seeds

SYRUP

¼ cup light corn syrup

4 tablespoons (½ stick) unsalted butter

2 tablespoons packed dark brown sugar

2 tablespoons honey

1 teaspoon fish sauce

½ teaspoon light soy sauce

½ teaspoon MSG

¼ teaspoon gochugaru (Korean chili flakes)

1 garlic clove, grated

JAMMY MARBLE TEA EGGS

MAKES 6 EGGS

My mom would often drop into a shop in Chinatown near my grandparents' apartment to buy tea eggs. The ones she bought had chalky yolks that turned a pale shade of green from a long soak in the simmering soy-spiced tea mixture. After an afternoon of grocery shopping, we liked to sit on my grandma's couch snacking on those eggs with a side of braised duck tongues. I would eat the tasty tea-stained whites and pass my mom the hard-cooked yolks. Traditional tea eggs have those firm yolks my mom loves so much, but I'm more partial to a nice jammy interior, so that's what I'm aiming for in this recipe.

1. In a small pot, combine 2 cups of the water, the star anise, cinnamon, ginger, dark and light soy sauces, tea leaves, wine, Szechuan and black peppercorns, and sugar. Place over high heat and bring to a boil. Once the mixture is boiling, cover the pot, reduce the heat to medium, and simmer for 15 minutes. (Covering the pot allows the spices and other flavorings to steep without all the water evaporating.)

2. Remove the marinade from the heat and pour into a shallow, small heatproof bowl and let cool for a few minutes. Transfer to the fridge to cool completely.

3. Fill a medium pot with water and bring to a boil over high heat. Using a slotted spoon, gently lower the eggs into the water and start a timer immediately for 7 minutes. If you prefer firmer yolks, like my mom does, boil the eggs for 11 minutes.

4. While the eggs cook, prepare an ice bath. Fill a medium bowl with equal parts ice and water.

5. When the eggs have finished cooking, using the slotted spoon, transfer the eggs to the ice bath, submerging them to stop the cooking. Once the eggs are cooled completely, remove them from the ice bath. Gently tap the shell of each egg with the back of a spoon to create small, spider web–like cracks all over, without removing any pieces of the shell.

6. Transfer the eggs to an 8½ × 4½-inch loaf pan (or even a rectangular take-out box) and lay a paper towel over the top. Pour in the black tea–soy marinade. The paper towel will allow the marinade to soak into the eggs if there's not enough marinade to submerge them. Cover the pan with plastic wrap and let the eggs marinate in the fridge for at least 12 hours and up to 18 before eating.

7. When you're ready to eat, peel the eggs and serve. Peel any eggs you plan to eat later and store in an airtight container in the fridge for up to 3 days.

2 cups water

2 star anise

1 cinnamon stick

1 (1-inch) piece ginger, sliced into 3 even pieces

5 tablespoons dark soy sauce

2 tablespoons light soy sauce

1 tablespoon loose leaf black tea (such as Ceylon, pekoe, or English breakfast; 2 to 3 tea bags)

1 tablespoon Shaoxing wine

1 teaspoon Szechuan peppercorns

1 teaspoon black peppercorns

1 teaspoon sugar

6 large eggs, at room temperature

TINNED DACE DIP

SERVES 6

This dip is dedicated to Troy from National Grid. Back in November of 2021, after months of patiently waiting for someone—anyone—to come turn the gas on at Bonnie's so we could finally open the restaurant to the public, we decided to pop up in our own space. Unceremoniously dubbed The No Gas Pop-Up, we packed the space full of old friends and family, new faces and neighbors, and served them dishes we never planned to have on the menu—shucked oysters dripping with gingery white peppercorn mignonette, clams on the half shell filled with an extra-scallop-heavy XO sauce, and this tinned dace dip: whipped fried dace with all the fermented black soybeans from the can, garlic chives, cream cheese, and sour cream. It's reminiscent of a chicken liver mousse and pairs perfectly with a Premium saltine. Two weeks later, Troy showed up to turn on our gas, and we opened the next week with this dish as the first thing our customers requested.

1. PREPARE THE DIP: Drain off and discard all the oil from both cans of dace, reserving the fish and all the soybeans.

2. In a food processor, combine the fish and soybeans and blitz until everything has broken down and formed a homogenous paste.

3. In a medium bowl, combine the blitzed dace, shallot, scallions, cream cheese, sour cream, mayonnaise, and sugar and mix well. Transfer to a serving dish, if serving immediately, or to an airtight container and refrigerate for up to 5 days.

4. TO SERVE: Garnish with the sesame seeds and scallion greens and serve with crackers or crudités.

DIP

2 (6.5- to 8-ounce) cans fried dace with fermented black soybeans

1 medium shallot, minced

3 scallions, thinly sliced

½ cup cream cheese, softened

3 tablespoons sour cream

1 tablespoon Kewpie mayonnaise

¼ teaspoon sugar

TO SERVE

1 tablespoon toasted white sesame seeds, to garnish

1 scallion, thinly sliced (green tops only)

1 sleeve salty or buttery crackers of your choice (I like Premium brand saltines) or Chinatown Crudités (page 106)

LEMON COLA CHICKEN WINGS

MAKES 24 WINGS

The cure for the common cold is lemon and ginger boiled with Coke. At least that's what my mom always told me. It also makes a wonderful base for a finger-licking, sticky-sweet sauce to coat chicken wings. The classic Cantonese cola wing recipe calls for braising the drums and flats with the lemon, ginger, and cola (and a hit of savory soy sauce) on the stovetop. As the chicken cooks, the sauce slowly reduces to a glaze. But I've always preferred a baked wing with lightly crisp skin under the syrupy glaze, so I'm tampering slightly with the traditional preparation but still delivering on that same irresistible, fun flavor combination.

1. Preheat the oven to 425°F. Line a large baking sheet with aluminum foil (for easy cleanup), then place an oven-safe wire rack in the pan.

2. PREPARE THE WINGS: Pat the chicken wings dry with paper towels and put them into a medium bowl. Drizzle with the oil, sprinkle with the salt, sugar, MSG, and baking soda, and toss until the wings are evenly coated.

3. Spread the wing pieces in an even layer on the prepared baking sheet. Bake for 40 minutes. Flip the pieces over and continue to bake until the exterior of each wing piece is golden brown all around and lightly crisp to the touch, about 10 minutes longer.

4. PREPARE THE GLAZE: While the wings are baking, heat a small pot over medium-high heat. Swirl in the oil, then add the ginger and scallions and toast, stirring every so often, until the aromatics take on a light golden color and are fragrant, about 5 minutes. Pour in the Coca-Cola, wine, soy sauce, and sugar and bring the mixture to a boil. Cook, stirring every 5 minutes, until the liquid is reduced by 75 percent and a thick, saucy glaze (think maple syrup consistency) forms, 25 to 30 minutes. Pour the glaze (you should have about ½ cup), including the ginger and scallions, into a medium heatproof bowl.

5. When the wings are ready, add them to the glaze and toss until each wing piece has a thin coating of sticky glaze with a little drippage. Plate the wings with the cooked pieces of ginger and scallion. Garnish the wings with the sesame seeds and finish with generous lemon squeezes.

WINGS

24 chicken wings (about 3 pounds), drums and flats separated, wing tips removed and discarded

2 tablespoons neutral oil, preferably grapeseed

2 teaspoons kosher salt

1 teaspoon sugar

1 teaspoon MSG

1 teaspoon baking soda

GLAZE

2 tablespoons neutral oil, preferably grapeseed

1 (4-inch) piece ginger, sliced into 6 even pieces

4 scallions, cut into 2-inch batons

2 (12-ounce) cans Coca-Cola

¼ cup Shaoxing wine

¼ cup light soy sauce

2 tablespoons sugar

1 tablespoon toasted white sesame seeds, to garnish

1 lemon, cut into 4 wedges, to serve

SHRIMP STICKS
with Ginger-Scallion Tartar Sauce

SERVES 3 OR 4

I'm well-versed in the world of after-school snacks—bags of Lay's Wavy and Ruffles Sour Cream & Onion, a cheese slice, a sack of tacos from Taco Bell, or a bucket of fried chicken from KFC. But the frozen fish sticks heated up in the toaster oven reigned supreme. I loved dipping them, crispy and flaky, in ketchup or mayo or both. This is an (ever-so-slightly) adult version of those beloved sticks from the yellow box but made from a basic shrimp paste studded with garlic chives and fresh ginger and dunked in a gingery scallion tartar sauce.

Blitzing the shrimp into a paste gives the shrimp sticks a smooth, bouncy bite, something that Cantonese folks crave. We love taking hunks of fish and shrimp and meat and whipping them into springy seasoned pastes with a light, airy texture perfect for fish balls and dim sum fillings and for shrimp sticks like these. It's a simple technique, and you can mix and match proteins however you wish. When I'm not making these shrimp sticks, I like to fold this shrimp paste into fatty ground pork for plump dumplings, or simply sear it off (almost like a crab cake) to eat over rice.

1. Line the bottom and sides of an 8½ x 4½-inch loaf pan with plastic wrap, leaving enough of an overhang on the long sides to cover the pan later.

2. PREPARE THE SHRIMP PASTE: In a food processor, combine the shrimp, egg, cornstarch, ginger, sesame oil, salt, MSG, sugar, baking soda, and pepper and blitz until a smooth paste forms. Add the chives and pulse four or five times to distribute them throughout the paste.

3. Scoop the shrimp paste into the prepared loaf pan and spread in an even layer. Cover with the overhang, then put the pan into the freezer and let the mixture set up until the center is firm to the touch, at least 2 hours. This will make the shrimp sticks much easier to work with when dredging and frying.

4. PREPARE THE GINGER-SCALLION TARTAR SAUCE: Meanwhile, in a small bowl, whisk together the mayonnaise, pickles, scallion sauce, vinegar, and salt. Cover and set aside in the fridge until ready to serve.

5. Once the shrimp paste is frozen into a block, pop the block out onto a cutting board and cut crosswise into ten even strips. This recipe is great for appetizer bites, so you could even cut the block into smaller, uniform cubes for a party.

SHRIMP PASTE

1 pound medium shrimp (U31/40), peeled and deveined

1 large egg

2 tablespoons cornstarch

1 tablespoon minced ginger

1 tablespoon toasted sesame oil

1 teaspoon kosher salt

½ teaspoon MSG

½ teaspoon sugar

¼ teaspoon baking soda

⅛ teaspoon ground white pepper

½ cup thinly sliced flat green garlic chives or scallions (green tops only)

GINGER-SCALLION TARTAR SAUCE

½ cup Kewpie mayonnaise

¼ cup minced pickles

¼ cup Green Chili Ginger Scallion Sauce (page 31)

1 tablespoon rice vinegar

⅛ teaspoon kosher salt

6. FRY THE SHRIMP STICKS: Pour oil to a depth of at least 2 inches (or halfway up the sides, whichever is shallower) into a large pot or Dutch oven and heat over medium-high heat to 350°F. Line a large plate with paper towels and set it near the stove.

7. While the oil heats, set up the dredging station. Put the cornstarch into a wide, shallow dish, the beaten eggs into another shallow dish, and the panko into a third shallow dish. Working in batches, dust the shrimp sticks with the cornstarch, shaking off the excess; then dip into the egg, letting the excess drip off; and finally, coat with the panko. Land the breaded shrimp sticks on a baking sheet until ready to fry.

8. Working in batches to avoid crowding, gently lower the breaded shrimp sticks into the oil and deep-fry, flipping halfway through, until golden brown on all sides, 5 to 6 minutes. Using a slotted spoon or spider, transfer to the paper towel–lined plate to drain. Repeat with the remaining shrimp sticks. Serve immediately with a big squeeze of lemon and the tartar sauce for dunking.

TO FRY

Neutral oil, preferably grapeseed

1 cup cornstarch

3 large eggs, beaten

2 cups panko breadcrumbs

Lemon wedges, to serve

SNACKS

SHRIMP COCKTAIL
with Fuyu Chive Aioli and Gingery Cocktail Sauce

MAKES 24 SHRIMP

I am an absolute sucker for a shrimp cocktail. If it's on the menu, I'm ordering it. If it's a passed snack at a wedding, I'm stalking the kitchen door waiting for a fully loaded fresh tray. If I'm catering an event, chances are I'm serving one. There's just something about that combination of delicately poached shrimp with a big hit of lemon and a tangy cocktail sauce that pleases almost everyone. If I have the time, I whip together this *fuyu* chive aioli. It's an extra-creamy savory element, perfect for double dipping.

Tip

If you're planning ahead for a party, poach the shrimp in the morning and pop them into the fridge until you serve later that night. I would not recommend poaching them a day ahead because the cooked shrimp can take on a mealy texture.

1. PREPARE THE FUYU CHIVE AIOLI: In a food processor, combine the mayonnaise, ketchup, ginger, garlic, lemon zest and juice, fuyu, pepper, salt, and MSG and pulse until a smooth, creamy texture forms. Transfer to a small bowl and fold in the garlic chives. Cover and set aside in the fridge until ready to serve.

2. PREPARE THE GINGERY COCKTAIL SAUCE: In a small bowl, whisk together the ketchup, horseradish, ginger, lemon juice, sriracha, soy sauce, and pepper, mixing well. Cover and set aside in the fridge until ready to serve.

3. PREPARE THE SHRIMP: Prepare an ice bath in a large bowl with equal parts ice and water. (See Tip.)

4. In a medium (5- to 8-quart) pot, combine the 10 cups water, the salt, sugar, and MSG. Squeeze the lemon halves over the pot, releasing the juice into the water, and then add the spent halves to the pot. Cover the pot, place over high heat, and bring to a boil. Once the liquid is at a roaring boil, add the shrimp, turn off the heat, and re-cover the pot. Poach the shrimp until they are no longer translucent and are cooked through, about 4 minutes.

5. Using a spider or slotted spoon, transfer the shrimp to the prepared ice bath to stop the cooking. Once the shrimp are fully cooled, gently peel and devein them, taking care to leave the tails on. Serve with the fuyu chive aioli and gingery cocktail sauce for dipping and the lemon wedges for an extra squeeze of juice.

FUYU CHIVE AIOLI

1 cup Kewpie mayonnaise

½ cup ketchup

1 (2-inch) piece ginger, sliced

2 garlic cloves, smashed

Grated zest and juice of 1 lemon

1 tablespoon fuyu (fermented bean curd) in chili (cube and liquid)

½ teaspoon freshly ground black pepper

⅛ teaspoon kosher salt

⅛ teaspoon MSG

¼ cup sliced flat green garlic chives or scallions (green tops only)

GINGERY COCKTAIL SAUCE

1½ cups ketchup

3 tablespoons prepared horseradish

3 tablespoons grated ginger

2 tablespoons freshly squeezed lemon juice

1 teaspoon sriracha

1 teaspoon light soy sauce

½ teaspoon freshly ground black pepper

SHRIMP

10 cups cold water

½ cup kosher salt

½ cup sugar

¼ cup MSG

2 lemons, halved, plus wedges for serving

24 jumbo shrimp (U16/20) in the shell, deveined

PORK AND CHIVE DUMPLINGS
with Caramelized Onion Soy Butter

SERVES 4 OR 5

To be honest, the first time I made this caramelized onion soy butter, I spooned it over store-bought dumplings. It's a play on the rich, sweet, oniony French sauce called soubise. To me, the perfect dumpling sauce should always have a good balance of soy and vinegar. And that combo, mixed with the depth and sweetness from these buttery caramelized onions, made a sauce that was better than any of the dipping sauces I had tucked away in the fridge. You don't actually have to make your own dumplings to make this caramelized onion soy butter. But if you're in the mood for a bit of a project, you certainly could. And if you really wanted to, you could double the quantity of the dumplings and throw one batch in your freezer for a quick meal down the road.

1. PREPARE THE CARAMELIZED ONION SOY BUTTER: In a small pot over medium-high heat, gently melt 3 tablespoons of the butter. When the butter foams, add the onions and stir until they begin to soften and brown. Reduce the heat to medium and cook, stirring frequently, until the onions are deeply golden brown and smelling sweet, 20 to 25 minutes.

2. Once the onions are jammy brown, transfer them to a blender, add the water, soy sauce, vinegar, and MSG, and blend on high speed until smooth. With the blender running on high speed, toss in the remaining cubes of cold butter, one at a time, until fully blended into a smooth, emulsified sauce. If the sauce breaks, add a touch more water, 1 teaspoon at a time, and blend on high speed until the sauce comes back together. Let cool to room temperature, then transfer to an airtight container and refrigerate until ready to serve. It will keep for up to 1 week.

3. PREPARE THE DUMPLING FILLING: In a small pot, bring 1 cup of the water to a boil over high heat. Put the mushrooms into a medium heatproof bowl and pour the boiling water over them. Set aside to soak and soften for 15 minutes. Drain off the water, remove and discard the stems, and coarsely chop the caps.

4. In a stand mixer fitted with the paddle attachment, combine the pork, garlic chives, ginger, cornstarch, salt, sugar, oyster sauce, sesame oil, pepper, baking soda, MSG, the remaining 1 teaspoon water, and the mushrooms. Mix on low speed until well blended, then whip on medium speed until a tacky, bouncy mixture forms, about 3 minutes. Set aside until you're ready to wrap the dumplings.

CARAMELIZED ONION SOY BUTTER

16 tablespoons (2 sticks) unsalted butter, cut into 1-tablespoon cubes and chilled, divided

2 white or yellow onions, thinly sliced

½ cup water

2 tablespoons light soy sauce

2 tablespoons rice vinegar

2 teaspoons MSG

DUMPLING FILLING

1 cup plus 1 teaspoon water, divided

5 dried shiitake mushrooms

¾ pound ground pork

1 cup thinly sliced flat green garlic chives or scallions (green tops only)

1 tablespoon minced ginger

1 teaspoon cornstarch

1 teaspoon kosher salt

1 teaspoon sugar

1 teaspoon oyster sauce

½ teaspoon toasted sesame oil

⅛ teaspoon freshly ground white pepper

⅛ teaspoon baking soda

⅛ teaspoon MSG

5. PREPARE THE DUMPLING DOUGH: In a medium bowl, combine the flour, boiling water, and salt. Using a rubber spatula, mix the ingredients together to form a shaggy dough. Cover the bowl with a large damp kitchen towel and let sit for 15 minutes to hydrate the flour.

6. Knead the shaggy mixture in the bowl until a supple soft dough forms, 3 to 5 minutes. Turn the dough out onto a clean work surface and, using your palms, roll into a 20-inch log. Using a knife, cut the log crosswise into forty even portions. If you have a kitchen scale, each piece should weigh around 10 grams. Keep all the dough portions under the damp kitchen towel so they don't dry out. Working in small batches, roll the dough portions into balls, then using a rolling pin, roll out each ball into a rough circle about 3 inches in diameter, with a thicker center and thinner edges. (You can use a round cookie cutter to shape up the edges if you want.) Lightly dust each dumpling round on both sides with flour before stacking on top of one another under the damp towel.

7. WRAP THE DUMPLINGS: Line a large baking sheet with parchment paper or plastic wrap. Fill a small bowl with room-temperature water. Set the baking sheet and the bowl near your work surface. Work with one wrapper at a time and keep the remaining wrappers covered with the damp towel to prevent the edges from drying out while you work. Scoop about ½ tablespoon of the filling onto the center of the dumpling wrapper. Dip your fingertip into the bowl of water and wet the edges of the wrapper. Fold the wrapper over to enclose the filling, creating a small half-moon. Press out any air bubbles and squeeze the edges together tightly to seal. Lay the finished dumpling on the prepared baking sheet.

8. Repeat with the remaining wrappers and filling and add them to the baking sheet. If you don't plan to eat all of the dumplings right away, freeze the extras on a baking sheet until fully frozen, then pop them into a ziplock bag and return them to the freezer for up to 1 month (and label with the date!).

9. To cook, fill a large pot with water, bring to a boil over high heat, and add the dumplings. (I usually like to serve eight to ten dumplings per person.) Boil the dumplings until they float to the surface, 8 minutes if fresh and 10 minutes if frozen. Remove the dumplings using a spider or slotted spoon.

10. Meanwhile, in a small pot over medium-low heat, gently reheat the caramelized onion soy butter until warm (¼ cup sauce for one serving of 8 to 10 dumplings is the perfect ratio in my opinion). Spoon the warmed sauce on the bottom of an individual serving dish and top with the dumplings. (If you have extra scallion and cilantro floating around your refrigerator crisper, use them to garnish the dumplings.)

DUMPLING DOUGH

2 cups (240g) all-purpose flour, plus more for dusting

⅔ cup (150g) boiling water

¼ teaspoon (3g) kosher salt

PIGGIES IN SCALLION MILK BREAD BLANKETS

SERVES 15 TO 20

Walk into any bakery in Chinatown to pick up a few treats, and you'll probably notice a stack of Chinese hot dog buns nestled in the display case next to sweet coconut and pineapple buns, fried fish sandwiches (page 221), and sponge cakes. Sometimes the dogs are shaped into beautiful flowers with a smattering of bright green scallions; other times they are simply wound with puffy blankets. They're delicious, but I've always been partial to the American cocktail-hour-snacking portion size—a one-biter to dunk into mustard while you mingle at fancy parties where you might not belong—so I like to slice up my milk bread–blanketed piggies into little bite-size pieces. And in my opinion, they are best served with a punchy, zingy Chinese hot honey mustard.

1. Line two baking sheets with parchment paper or nonstick baking mats.

2. PREPARE THE BLANKETS: Punch down the dough, then turn out onto a work surface lightly dusted with flour. Divide the dough into twelve even pieces. If you have a kitchen scale, each piece should weigh about 55 grams. The dough should be tacky to the touch, but if it feels too sticky to handle, lightly flour your hands. Roll each piece out into a thin 15- to 17-inch-long log.

3. PREPARE THE PIGGIES: Pat the hot dogs dry with paper towels, then roll the dogs in flour to lightly coat the sides, tapping off any excess. This will help the dough stick. Coil the milk bread logs over each hot dog, starting from one end, wrapping until you reach the other end, and leaving roughly ½ inch of the dogs exposed on each end so steam can escape when the piggies bake. Repeat with the remaining dough logs and hot dogs. As you work, divide the piggies evenly between the prepared baking sheets, placing six piggies on each baking sheet and spacing them 2 to 3 inches apart. Loosely cover the pans with plastic wrap and let the piggies proof for 40 to 45 minutes at room temperature. They are ready to bake when the blankets are puffed up but hold a small imprint when poked.

4. While the blankets proof, position two racks in the middle of the oven and preheat to 350°F.

MILK BREAD BLANKETS

Milk bread dough (page 60), prepared through step 4

All-purpose flour, to dust

PIGGIES

12 hot dogs

All-purpose flour, to dust

1 large egg

1 tablespoon whole milk

3 scallions, thinly sliced

2 tablespoons toasted white sesame seeds

1 tablespoon Maldon flaky salt

5. To make an egg wash, in a small bowl whisk together the egg and milk until there are no streaks of egg. Brush the egg wash over the tops and crevices of the blankets, then sprinkle evenly with the scallions, sesame seeds, and flaky salt. Bake the piggies, switching the pans between the racks and rotating them back to front halfway through, until the blankets are lightly golden brown, 22 to 25 minutes. Remove from the oven and transfer the piggies to the racks and let cool completely.

6. PREPARE THE HOT HONEY MUSTARD: In a small bowl, whisk together the honey and hot water until the honey dissolves. Whisk in the mustard, mixing well.

7. TO SERVE: Slice each piggy into five even pieces. Serve with the hot honey mustard alongside for dipping.

HOT HONEY MUSTARD

½ cup honey

1 tablespoon hot water

½ cup Chinese Hot Mustard (page 30)

SNACKS

YAUH JA GWAI
(Fried Crullers)

MAKES 4 CRULLERS

Airy, deep-fried *yauh ja gwai*—literally translated to "oil-fried ghosts"—go by many names, including fried dough sticks, *youtiao*, and fried crullers. It's hard to miss a stack of these fluffy, golden dough sticks piled up on the counter at just about every shop selling tofu or roast meats or congee or dim sum in Chinatown. They are the ultimate congee dunkers and sauce-sopper-uppers. I pick some up every time I go shopping and always keep a stack in my freezer to flash in the oven for a superquick reheat that crisps up the exterior but keeps that soft, squishy interior. You can usually grab them at Asian markets or restaurants in Chinatown. Chances are if a spot sells congee, it will sell you *yauh ja gwai*. (You can even buy them online.) But they're also easy to make at home with ingredients you probably already have lying around. Serve with congee (pages 143 and 144) or slice into chunks to use in Yauh Ja Gwai Panzanella (page 110) or stir-fry with *dao gok* (page 117).

1. PREPARE THE DOUGH: In a stand mixer fitted with the dough hook, mix together the flour, baking powder, baking soda, salt, and sugar on low speed until blended. In a small bowl, whisk together the egg, water, and oil, mixing well.

2. With the mixer running on low speed, slowly stream the wet ingredients into the dry ingredients. Increase the mixer speed to medium and knead the dough (if at first the dry ingredients aren't incorporated, use a rubber spatula along the edge of the bowl to encourage mixing) until it comes together and is smooth, about 10 minutes. The dough should be a little sticky to the touch. Cover the bowl with plastic wrap and let the dough rest and relax at room temperature for 30 minutes.

3. Turn the dough out onto a work surface lightly dusted with flour. Using your hands, gently press the dough into a rectangle roughly 9 inches long, 7 inches wide, and ¼ inch thick. Tightly wrap the dough rectangle in plastic wrap and lay it flat on a baking sheet. Pop the pan into the fridge and let the dough rest for 4 to 6 hours.

2 cups (240g) all-purpose flour, plus more for dusting

1 teaspoon (3g) baking powder

½ teaspoon (3g) baking soda

½ teaspoon (3g) kosher salt

½ teaspoon (2g) sugar

1 large egg

½ cup (113g) water

1 tablespoon (12g) neutral oil, preferably grapeseed, plus more for frying

RECIPE CONTINUES

4. SHAPE THE YAUH JA GWAI: Work with the dough while it is cold so it's easier to handle. Lightly dust the work surface again with flour and lay the dough rectangle on it. Cut the rectangle crosswise into eight even strips each about 1 inch wide. Lift one strip and stack it, unfloured side down, on top of a second strip. Press the strips together so they stick to each other. Repeat with the remaining strips to make four dough sticks total. Working with one dough stick at a time, use a chopstick to press firmly into the center of each stick, creating the iconic vertical crease down the middle. This will help join the stacked dough pieces together into one stick. If the chopstick sticks, lightly grease it with oil before each creasing. Cover the dough sticks with plastic wrap after shaping to prevent them from drying out.

5. PREPARE TO FRY: Pour oil to a depth of at least 2 inches (or halfway up the sides, whichever is shallower) of a large pot or Dutch oven (10 to 12 inches in diameter) and heat over medium-high heat to 375°F to 400°F. Line a large plate with paper towels and set it near the stove.

6. FRY THE YAUH JA GWAI: When the oil is ready, working with one dough stick at a time, carefully stretch it to roughly 10 inches long, then gently lower it into the oil. Fry the dough stick, flipping it nonstop with tongs or chopsticks to ensure it fries evenly, until it puffs up and turns lightly golden brown, about 1 minute. Transfer to the paper towel–lined plate to drain. Repeat with the remaining dough sticks.

7. Serve the yauh ja gwai hot. To store, let cool, pop them into a ziplock bag, and refrigerate for up to 1 week or freeze for up to 1 month. To reheat, place on a wire rack set in a baking sheet, transfer to a preheated 400°F oven, and heat until warmed through and crispy again, about 6 minutes.

SNACKS

3
VEGETABLES

The blocks of Manhattan's Chinatown are imprinted in my mind from years of chasing after my mom. The map in my head is made up of roast meat shops and vegetable vendors and bakeries and *cheung fun* (rice noodle rolls) street carts. We would jostle our way through the streets to shop where she knew she could haggle the best deals, find the best ingredients. We didn't talk very much during those hours, but she taught me how to tackle the produce aisle in the grocery store like a seasoned professional: to shop with the vegetable sales, not the seasons; to be mindful and resourceful as you shop and to save food containers for storage and organization; and to use every last bit of a vegetable.

A Guide to Cantonese Vegetables	104
Chinatown Crudités with Sour Cream and Green Onion Dip	106
Cabbage Salad with Fried Garlic Sesame Dressing	109
Yauh Ja Gwai Panzanella	110
Hot Salad	113
Charred Cabbage with Shrimp Paste Butter	114
Dao Gok with Fermented Bean Curd Garlic Butter	117
Crispy Ham and Cheese Lo Bak Go	118
Mommy Knows Best	121
Steamed Egg Custard with Vinegary, Marinated Tomatoes	122
Corn Chowder	126
Cantonese Minestrone	128

A Guide to Cantonese Vegetables

Whenever I'm shopping for vegetables, I have two options: the Chinese supermarket and the street vendor stalls. Chinese supermarkets are stocked with both Chinese and Western vegetables: Chinese broccoli and broccolini, Chinese cauliflower and Western cauliflower, *dao gok* and string beans, and every variety of cabbage. And beyond vegetables, they have everything you need to stock your pantry (page 17), roasted meats, fish tanks full of fresh seafood, whole freezer sections packed

with frozen noodles and dumplings, and a "valet system" by the entrance for the aunties to stash their rolling shopping bags. Chinese supermarkets are a one-stop shop.

You'll find pockets of street vendors and little market stalls spilling out onto the sidewalks throughout Manhattan's Chinatown. Often, the produce sold by these vendors is incredibly seasonal and fresh. Take your time perusing the streets. The price per pound and produce quality may be much better just a few stalls down. Go early for the good stuff but know that whatever veggies vendors don't sell by the end of the day, they start foisting

1. CHINESE BROCCOLI
2. DAO GOK
3. CHINESE CELERY

on unsuspecting customers with the lure of steep discounts. And with parking so hard to come by, I occasionally like to treat the street vendors almost like a drive-through. I drive up to a long stretch of stalls, throw my hazards on, jump out of the car, stuff bags full of bok choy and budding garlic chives, pay in cash, jump back in the car, drive a little farther down the block, and do it all over again. The meter maids of New York City rarely catch me.

If you don't happen to have quick access to a local Chinatown or Asian market, don't stress too much. There are substitutions for just about every vegetable in this book. While broccolini as a substitute for Chinese broccoli may not be identical in flavor and texture, that shouldn't deter you from making the Clay Pot Rice (Without a Clay Pot) on page 150. After all, recipes are meant to be just a guide, not a constraint. (And I won't be offended, as I rarely follow a recipe as is.) So take a look at the ingredient lists, and if you can't source the first vegetable, give the recommended Western counterpart a try.

4. DAIKON
5. CHINESE CAULIFLOWER
6. GARLIC CHIVES

VEGETABLES

CHINATOWN CRUDITÉS
with Sour Cream and Green Onion Dip

SERVES 4 TO 6

Cantonese people don't eat a whole lot of cold, raw vegetables. We love our vegetables ripping hot—stir-fried or deep-fried, steamed or blanched. So I've never really liked a carrot stick or cucumber spear all that much. I do like a good dip, though. And a crunchy vegetable is a great way to shovel lots of dip into my body. You can play around with whatever vegetables happen to be in season for this crudités platter. But no matter what, definitely plate those veggies up with a few fistfuls of potato chips and a bowl of sour cream and green onion (also known as scallion) dip on the side.

1. PREPARE THE SOUR CREAM AND GREEN ONION DIP: In a medium pot over medium-high heat, melt the butter. When the butter foams, add the onions and cook, stirring, until they begin to soften and brown, about 7 to 8 minutes. Reduce the heat to medium and continue to cook, stirring frequently, until the onions are deeply golden brown and smelling sweet, 20 to 25 minutes. Transfer the caramelized onions to a small bowl and set aside to cool to room temperature.

2. In a medium bowl, combine the sour cream, mayonnaise, cream cheese, scallions, lemon juice, garlic, onion powder, salt, pepper, and MSG and stir to mix well. Coarsely chop the cooled caramelized onions, add to the sour cream mixture, and mix well. Cover and refrigerate until ready to serve. The dip will keep in an airtight container in the fridge for up to 3 days.

3. FOR THE CHINATOWN CRUDITÉS: In a medium pot, combine 6 cups of the water and the salt and bring to a rolling boil over high heat. While the water heats, prepare an ice bath in a large bowl with equal parts ice and water.

4. When the water is boiling, blanch the vegetables in batches: Blanch the dao gok and Chinese cauliflower together for 30 seconds, then, using a spider, immediately transfer them to the ice bath to stop the cooking. Blanch the carrots for 1 minute, then use the spider to transfer them to the ice bath to stop the cooking.

5. Remove the dao gok, cauliflower, and carrots from the ice bath and lay them on a kitchen towel to pat dry.

6. TO SERVE: Arrange the blanched dao gok, cauliflower, and carrots and the raw snap peas and celery on a serving plate. Accompany with bowls of the dip and the potato chips.

SOUR CREAM AND GREEN ONION DIP

2 tablespoons unsalted butter

2 small yellow onions, sliced

1 cup sour cream

½ cup Kewpie mayonnaise

¼ cup cream cheese, at room temperature

3 scallions, thinly sliced

2 tablespoons freshly squeezed lemon juice

1 garlic clove, minced

½ tablespoon onion powder

1½ teaspoons kosher salt

½ teaspoon freshly ground black pepper

½ teaspoon MSG

CHINATOWN CRUDITÉS

6 cups water

½ cup kosher salt

½ pound dao gok, cut into 6- to 7-inch pieces with the stems removed, or string beans, left whole

½ pound Chinese cauliflower or Western cauliflower florets with stems

½ pound small rainbow carrots, halved lengthwise

¼ pound snap peas or snow peas

3 stalks Chinese celery or celery with leaves, cut into 6-inch pieces

2 cups potato chips

CABBAGE SALAD
with Fried Garlic Sesame Dressing

SERVES 4

The star (not-so-secret) ingredient in this super-simple salad dressing is bits of fried garlic. You can't develop a deep garlicky taste with grated raw garlic or a dash of garlic powder. You need deep-fried, lightly golden pieces of garlic. Luckily, you don't have to fry them yourself. That would be immensely time-consuming and completely unnecessary, especially when you can buy at the Asian supermarket massive jars of the stuff that are perfect every time. More often than not, fried garlic is used as a simple garnish, but I like to sneak the fried allium into this creamy vegan dressing for an extra punch of flavor.

1. PREPARE THE GARNISH: In a spice grinder or mortar and pestle, combine the sesame seeds and shallots and pulse a few times to a crushed, sandy texture. Pour the garnish into a small bowl and set aside.

2. PREPARE THE DRESSING: In the same blender (no need to rinse it or wipe it out), combine the tofu, water, vinegar, tahini, fried garlic, salt, and MSG. Starting on low speed, slowly blend the dressing while gradually increasing the speed to high, continuing to blend until the mixture is smooth and creamy. You should have about 1½ cups dressing. This dressing can be made up to a week ahead and stored in an airtight container in the fridge. It can also be used as a dipping sauce!

3. DRESS THE GREENS: In a large bowl, toss the cabbage with the dressing to coat evenly. Feel free to use as much or as little dressing as you like. Gently massage the cabbage with your hands until tender. Season the greens with salt and MSG to taste. Garnish with the crushed sesame-shallot mixture and serve.

GARNISH

1 tablespoon toasted white sesame seeds

1 tablespoon store-bought fried shallots

DRESSING

½ pound soft tofu (not silken), drained

6 tablespoons water

¼ cup rice vinegar

2 tablespoons tahini

2 tablespoons store-bought fried garlic

1 teaspoon kosher salt

½ teaspoon MSG

GREENS

1 pound savoy, or purple or white napa cabbage leaves, roughly cut into 1-inch pieces

Kosher salt

MSG

YAUH JA GWAI PANZANELLA

SERVES 6

The key to a good panzanella is the bread: toasty dried (but not necessarily stale) cubes that turn lightly soggy as they absorb all the juices of fresh, summery produce. I always thought *yauh ja gwai* could be the perfect crouton. And while I do love the crunch of a fresh fried dough stick, I love the extra-flavorful soggy bites when it's dunked into congee even more. So it only made sense to swap the bread in panzanella for chunks of cruller, toasting them off before tossing them with juicy heirloom tomatoes and stone fruit. At the end of the day, panzanella is just a bread salad with some other tasty bits mixed in, so you better choose that bread wisely. And I'll choose *yauh ja gwai* any day.

1. Fill a medium bowl with water, add the mustard greens, and let soak for 30 minutes. Drain the mustard greens and discard the soaking liquid. Wrap the greens in a paper towel and squeeze out any residual water. Set aside.

2. While the mustard greens soak, preheat the oven to 400°F. Lay the cruller pieces in a single layer on a baking sheet. When the oven is ready, slide the pan into the oven and toast the pieces for 6 to 8 minutes. They will crisp up slightly and take on a little color. Set aside to cool.

3. In a large bowl, combine the tomatoes, salt, and MSG and toss to coat the tomatoes evenly. Set aside for 15 minutes to draw out the tomato juices.

4. In a small bowl, whisk together the oil, vinegar, mustard, garlic, and pepper to make a dressing.

5. Add the cooled cruller pieces, mustard greens, apricots, peaches, mozzarella, cilantro, and scallions to the large bowl with the tomatoes. Pour in all of the dressing and toss well to mix evenly. Cover and refrigerate for at least 1 hour and preferably up to 3 hours.

6. When ready to serve, pull the panzanella from the fridge and toss to redistribute the dressing and tomato juices. Tear the basil leaves into pieces and scatter them on top to garnish.

1 cup drained and coarsely chopped pickled mustard greens

4 cups chopped yauh ja gwai (page 98; about 2 crullers), cut into ½-inch pieces

5 medium heirloom tomatoes, cut into large dice (about 6 cups)

1 tablespoon kosher salt

1 teaspoon MSG

6 tablespoons extra-virgin olive oil

3 tablespoons rice vinegar

2 teaspoons Dijon mustard

3 garlic cloves, finely minced

½ teaspoon freshly ground black pepper

2 ripe apricots, pitted and thinly sliced

2 ripe yellow peaches, pitted and thinly sliced

1½ cups drained *ciliegine* (cherry-size fresh mozzarella balls), quartered

½ cup chopped fresh cilantro

3 scallions, thinly sliced

6 fresh basil leaves, to garnish

HOT SALAD

SERVES 2

I often go grocery shopping with lofty expectations for the week ahead—far too many cuts of meat for our three-person family, way too many veggies for our toddler who eats only berries and chicken nuggets, and just too much lettuce considering that we never bother making salads. This salad is the exception. It's the fastest and tastiest way to use up the sad heads of romaine tucked away at the back of our crisper after another poor attempt at meal planning. The lettuce gets a quick stir-fry, so it remains crisp and crunchy, but it takes on a bit of char in the smoking-hot pan. This is about as classic as a stir-fry can be, and you can swap in pretty much any leafy green in place of romaine. Think bok choy, napa cabbage, pea shoots, kale, *yu choy*, or Swiss chard. And the best part is it will taste almost exactly like the veg you get under a pile of *cha siu* (page 212) or roast duck from the roast meat shops in Chinatown.

1. Heat the neutral oil in a 10- to 12-inch cast-iron skillet over high heat. Once the oil is shimmering, add the garlic and toss quickly to flavor the oil without burning the garlic, about 15 seconds. The garlic should be lightly browned.

2. Add half of the romaine and quickly stir to coat it with the oil, then leave undisturbed until the leaves start to char, about 2 minutes. Once the leaves are wilted, add the remaining romaine, the seasoned soy sauce, and the oyster sauce and toss to mix well. Continue stir-frying until the liquid is slightly reduced and the lettuce is cooked through and wilted but the stemmy fibrous parts still have a bit of crunch, about 2 minutes.

3. Remove the pan from the heat, drizzle the lettuce with the sesame oil and sprinkle with the salt and pepper. Toss to mix well, then serve immediately.

2 tablespoons neutral oil, preferably grapeseed

2 garlic cloves, smashed

1 large head romaine lettuce, roughly chopped into 1-inch pieces

1 tablespoon Seasoned Soy Sauce (page 35) or sweet soy sauce (I like Lee Kum Kee brand)

1 tablespoon oyster sauce

¼ teaspoon toasted sesame oil

¼ teaspoon kosher salt

⅛ teaspoon freshly ground white pepper

VEGETABLES

CHARRED CABBAGE
with Shrimp Paste Butter

SERVES 6

If you haven't noticed yet, I'm a lover of overly salty things. Really savory, salty things. Especially fermenty, savory, salty things like shrimp paste. It's one of those extremely flavorful and pungent condiments that lends the kind of depth to a dish that a few extra pinches of salt can never achieve. A little shrimp paste goes a long, long, long way. My mom taught me that. It's insanely good brushed over leftover roast pork or fried in a wok with cabbage and dried shrimp. Or better yet, fold it into a bit of butter, slather it over chunks of cabbage, and roast off until the charred cabbage and buttery shrimp paste flavors meld into wonderfully salty bites.

1. Preheat the oven to 450°F.

2. In a small bowl, combine the butter, garlic, shrimp paste, and sugar. Using the back of a spoon or a rubber spatula, squish everything together to make a shrimp paste compound butter. Set aside.

3. Remove and discard the rough outer leaves of the cabbage. Cut the half head of cabbage through the stem into even wedges. Drizzle each piece with 1 tablespoon of the oil, making sure to coat all the exposed leaves. In a small bowl, mix together the salt, MSG, and pepper. Evenly season the cut sides of the cabbage with the mixture.

4. Heat a 12-inch cast-iron skillet over high heat, then add the remaining 2 tablespoons oil. When the oil is shimmering, reduce the heat to medium-high and sear the flat side of each cabbage wedge until charred, about 3 minutes on each side.

5. Remove the pan from the heat and slather the flat sides of the cabbage wedges with the shrimp paste compound butter. Pour in the water around the edge of the pan (you don't want any water to hit the crispy cabbage leaves). Transfer the pan to the oven and roast the cabbage until the center is tender and fully cooked through and the blade of a sharp knife pierces through the cabbage with little to no resistance, about 25 minutes.

6. Transfer the cabbage to a platter. Pour the pan drippings over the wedges and serve immediately.

4 tablespoons (½ stick) unsalted butter, at room temperature

2 garlic cloves, grated

2 teaspoons fermented shrimp paste

¼ teaspoon sugar

½ large head green cabbage

4 tablespoons neutral oil, preferably grapeseed, divided

½ teaspoon salt

½ teaspoon MSG

⅛ teaspoon freshly ground white pepper

½ cup water

DAO GOK
with Fermented Bean Curd Garlic Butter

SERVES 2

My grandma had the most impressive green thumb. Every spring and summer she transformed our drab concrete Brooklyn backyard into tall rows of greenery: wispy tomato vines growing up and over my head, bitter melon and winter melon, and my absolute favorite, *dao gok*. They're often referred to as Chinese long beans, and the ones she grew were long, long, looooooong. The *dao gok* slithered all the way up the fence in my backyard, snaking along the edge of the garden and into the neighbors' yards. We had so many beans, my mom would drop off bundles of them on her friends' doorsteps just so we didn't have to eat them for every meal. You can treat *dao gok* like regular old string beans for a simple veggie side dish. But at the restaurant, I like to toss them in this fermented bean curd garlic butter along with big chunks of doughy *yauh ja gwai* to soak up the compound butter like garlic bread.

1. In a small bowl, combine the butter, fuyu, garlic, salted radish, and sugar. Using the back of a spoon or a rubber spatula, squish everything together to make a compound butter. Set aside.

2. Trim about 1 inch off the stem end of each long bean. Cut the long beans into 4- to 5-inch pieces. If using string beans, just trim the ends.

3. Lay a kitchen towel on a baking sheet and set near the stove. In a small pot, bring the water to a boil over high heat. Add the beans and blanch for 1 minute. Using a spider or tongs, transfer the beans to the towel to drain.

4. Heat the oil in a large cast-iron or carbon-steel skillet over high heat. Once the oil is shimmering, add the blanched beans and char, stirring once or twice, for 1 to 2 minutes. They should take on a bit of color.

5. Add the cruller pieces and compound butter to the beans and toss until the butter is well incorporated. Season with the salt and MSG and toss to finish. Serve immediately topped with crushed fried shallot, if using.

2 tablespoons unsalted butter, at room temperature

1 tablespoon fuyu (fermented bean curd) in chili (cube and liquid)

3 garlic cloves, minced

2 teaspoons minced salted radish

⅛ teaspoon sugar

½ pound dao gok or string beans

4 cups water

2 teaspoons neutral oil, preferably grapeseed

1 cup chopped yauh ja gwai (page 98; about ½ cruller), cut into ½-inch pieces

⅛ teaspoon kosher salt

⅛ teaspoon MSG

2 tablespoons fried shallot, crushed (optional)

VEGETABLES

CRISPY HAM AND CHEESE LO BAK GO

SERVES 4 TO 6

Turnip cake, daikon cake, radish cake, carrot cake—these are all names for the same savory dim sum staple, *lo bak go*. At its core, *lo bak go* is a mound of grated daikon mixed with a bit of cured pork, oftentimes Chinese sausage, and dried shrimp; pressed into a firm brick; steamed until delightfully springy yet soft; and then crisped up along the edges in a hot pan. My mom, in her usual spirit of no waste, taught me to reserve the water from the shredded daikon. Rather than pour that liquid down the drain, she whisked it with rice flour into a slurry to thicken the steamed cake and fortify it with the mildly earthy and sweet daikon flavor. She further reinforced that radishy flavor with bits of salted radish. But folded into this turnip-cake recipe are two new additions, salty chunks of country ham and shredded Gruyère cheese that turns gooey and stretchy—reminiscent of the ham and cheese sandwiches I made for myself in elementary school in an effort to fit in better with everyone else.

1. Peel the daikon, grate on the largest holes of a box grater, and transfer to a medium bowl. Sprinkle with the salt and set aside for at least 30 minutes or up to 1 hour to draw out the water.

2. Grease a 8½ × 4½-inch loaf pan with a bit of oil.

3. After 30 minutes to 1 hour, a good amount of water will have leached out of the grated daikon into the bowl. Pour the leached water into a large measuring cup. Wrap the daikon in a kitchen towel and wring out as much of the remaining water as possible into the measuring cup. Reserve 1 cup of the liquid and the grated daikon separately. The rest of the liquid can be discarded.

4. In a medium-to-large bowl, make a slurry by whisking together the rice flour and the reserved daikon water until smooth.

5. Heat the oil in a large sauté pan over medium-high heat. Once the oil is shimmering, add the ham, garlic, scallions, and salted radish and cook, stirring often to prevent any browning, until the aromatics are fragrant and soft, about 5 minutes. Add the wrung-out daikon to the mixture and cook to draw out any remaining moisture, stirring often to prevent any browning, until the mixture is fragrant and soft, about 3 minutes. Reduce the heat to low and pour in the slurry around the edge of the pan. Then, using a rubber spatula, stir and scrape the mixture constantly until it becomes a very thick, gloopy mixture and almost hard to stir. This should happen in about 3 minutes.

HAM AND CHEESE LO BAK GO

2 pounds daikon radishes
  or white turnips

1 tablespoon kosher salt

3 tablespoons neutral oil, preferably
  grapeseed, plus more for greasing
  the pan

1 cup rice flour

1 cup finely diced country ham

5 garlic cloves, minced

3 scallions, thinly sliced

2 tablespoons chopped salted radish

2 cups shredded Gruyère cheese

1 teaspoon MSG

¼ teaspoon freshly ground black pepper

6. Remove the pan from the heat and fold in the cheese, MSG, and pepper until evenly distributed. Scrape the daikon mixture into the prepared loaf pan, pressing with the back of the spatula to create an even, firm block.

7. In a large pot, bring a steamer setup (see page 43) to a rapid simmer over medium-high heat. Carefully lower the loaf pan onto the steaming rack. Cover and steam the daikon mixture until the edges become slightly opaque and the cake is firm to the touch, about 45 minutes.

8. Remove the loaf pan from the steamer setup and set aside until the daikon cake cools to room temperature, 45 minutes to 1 hour. When cool, unmold it onto a cutting board and portion the cake into twelve even slices. Store any slices you don't plan to eat right away in an airtight container in the fridge for up to 3 days.

9. TO SERVE: In a large sauté pan, melt 1 tablespoon butter over medium heat. When the butter foams, add as many daikon cake slices to the pan as will fit without crowding and press down firmly to sear on the first side until crispy and golden brown, about 4 minutes. Flip the slices, press down firmly, and sear until the second side is crispy and golden brown, about 4 minutes longer. Transfer to a plate and repeat with the remaining slices. I like to serve two slices per person. Serve with the chili oil and hot mustard on the side for dipping, if using, and eat immediately.

TO SERVE

Unsalted butter, for searing

Shrimp Chili Oil (page 36) or store-bought chili oil (optional)

Chinese Hot Mustard (page 30), optional

VEGETABLES

MOMMY KNOWS BEST

Every night without fail, my mom prepared feasts for our family.

She cooked the simple yet nuanced food she grew up eating. She loved a steamed egg custard or whole fish, a simple wok-tossed veggie, a pot of rice, and a salty preserved egg. She was, and still is, an amazing cook. She's natural, intuitive, resourceful, and never, ever wasteful. Everything I know about Cantonese food, I learned from watching her in the kitchen over the years.

I loved watching my mom pull together these spreads. I would rush through my homework after school just so I could stand at the counter and watch her cook, assisting when she'd allow. She kept all of her recipes and newspaper clippings stapled in a green-and-white-marbled school notebook. She never really followed the instructions. She relied more on her instincts and whatever we had hiding in the pantry. She used a cleaver exclusively to slice, dice, and smash. None of her cooking equipment was fancy or high-end. Oftentimes she used pots and pans with lids and handles missing. She built an oil-splatter guard for the wok out of cardboard wrapped in excessive layers of aluminum foil. She worked with what she had. And she made it work well.

All the food I cook now is rooted in those same Cantonese flavors. When I was developing dishes for this book, I constantly turned to my mom for inspiration. She would spend hours scouring WeChat and YouTube in Chinese for videos, articles, anything that could help me. She tapped into a whole different world I could have never found on my own. She would send voice notes with translations for me, knowing my Cantonese could use some brushing up. She would have suggestions about which shops in Chinatown to check for specialty ingredients and what brands to look out for. Every little tip helped. Every little piece of information she shared with me made my food better.

VEGETABLES

STEAMED EGG CUSTARD
with Vinegary, Marinated Tomatoes

SERVES 2

I learned how to make steamed egg custard from my mom. She rarely measures ingredients. Her technique for this dish utilizes eggshells to measure the proper ratio of liquid to egg to yield the most velvety-smooth consistency. And while that works well, I tend to follow more precise mathematical measurements, along with three crucial steps, to achieve the perfect texture time and time again. Number one, use a steaming tray or an even, flat-bottomed plate to ensure the custard cooks consistently throughout. Number two, remove as many of the air bubbles as possible from the surface of the custard base before wrapping the tray extremely tightly with plastic wrap. Number three, don't skimp on the plastic wrap. The plastic wrap is there to catch all the condensation that would otherwise drip onto the custard before it finishes steaming, causing blemishes and an undesirably rough texture.

This is a dish where less is more, and any additions you make might take away from the texture of the custard, which is perfectly silky on its own. Once you get the egg custard base down, you can play around with other flavors and toppings beyond these vinegary marinated tomatoes (tiny tomato tangent: I know they aren't technically vegetables, but everyone thinks they are, so that's why this recipe is in this chapter). Drizzle a bit of soy over the plain custard and garnish with a handful of herbs or spoon on heaps of Black Bean Garlic Sauce (page 28). For a seafoody twist, you can try nestling clams in the custard base before steaming.

Note

If you want to take these marinated tomatoes a step further (and get a little cheffy), keep the tomatoes whole and throw them onto a baking sheet. Then use a kitchen torch to char the skins on the tomatoes. Once the tomatoes are charred, gently peel off the skins and rinse briefly under cold running water. (If you don't have a torch, score a tiny X on the bottom of each tomato, dunk the tomatoes in boiling water for 15 seconds, shock them in an ice bath, and then, using a paring knife, peel away the tomato skin.) Although this peeling step may seem unnecessary, the texture of a peeled tomato, which absorbs the oil-and-vinegar marinade, is particularly satisfying when eaten along with the silky egg custard.

RECIPE AND INGREDIENTS CONTINUE

1. PREPARE THE MARINATED TOMATOES: In a small bowl, toss together the tomatoes, olive oil, vinegar, salt, sugar, and MSG, mixing well. Set aside to marinate while you prepare and steam the egg custard.

2. PREPARE THE EGG CUSTARD: In a large measuring cup, whisk the eggs until homogenous. There should be nothing but golden egg—no streaks. Take note of how much beaten egg you have in the measuring cup. You should have about 1 cup (8 fluid ounces). Multiply the quantity of beaten egg by 1.5 to determine the amount of water you need to add, which is usually about 1½ cups (12 fluid ounces). Whisk in that calculated amount of water, then whisk in the salt and MSG.

3. Set a fine-mesh strainer over a 7- to 9-inch steaming tray and pass the egg mixture through the strainer to remove any stray egg-white clumps or shell bits. Use a spoon to gently skim and discard any bubbles on top.

4. Lay a long sheet of plastic wrap on the counter, then gently place the custard-filled steaming tray on one end of the plastic wrap. Bring the remaining plastic wrap over the top of the tray to meet the bottom in one continuous tight sheet. Wrap as tightly as possible to prevent moisture from getting in.

5. In a large pot, bring a steamer setup (see page 43) to a rapid simmer over medium-high heat. Carefully lower the steaming tray onto the steaming rack. Cover and steam the egg custard for 10 minutes. Be patient and wait the full 10 minutes before lifting the lid to check on the custard. You're looking for the top of the custard to be smooth and uniform, with a tiny jiggle under the surface. Remove the tray from the steamer setup and allow it to rest for 1 minute before removing the plastic wrap.

6. Gently pour the marinated tomatoes over the egg custard. Drizzle the whole dish with sesame oil to finish before serving.

MARINATED TOMATOES

1 cup assorted cherry tomatoes or Sungold tomatoes (see Note, page 122)

1 tablespoon extra-virgin olive oil

1 tablespoon sherry vinegar

¼ teaspoon kosher salt

⅛ teaspoon sugar

⅛ teaspoon MSG

Toasted sesame oil, to drizzle

STEAMED EGG CUSTARD

4 large eggs

1 teaspoon kosher salt

½ teaspoon MSG

VEGETABLES

CORN CHOWDER

SERVES 4 TO 6

My family loves corn on the cob. In the height of corn season, we would boil the ears until the kernels were plump and bright yellow before slathering butter into all the tiny crevices. My grandma always poured off the corn boiling liquid into dainty teacups to sip on like a light corn broth after dinner. She never liked to waste. This chunky corn chowder leans heavily on that no-waste mentality deeply ingrained into my family's psyche. Rather than throw away the cobs after removing the kernels, stir them into the soup to reinforce that sweet corn flavor. And maybe spend an extra minute scraping out every last bit of the golden corn milk from the cobs before tossing them for good.

1. In a medium pot over medium heat, melt the butter. Add the onion, ginger, and garlic and allow to sweat, stirring often to prevent any browning, until the aromatics are fragrant and soft, about 5 minutes. Add the corn kernels and cook, stirring occasionally, until the kernels start to soften and take on a little color, 2 to 3 minutes. Season with the sugar, salt, MSG, white pepper, and black pepper.

2. Sprinkle the aromatics and corn with the flour and, using a rubber spatula, stir until the buttery moisture is absorbed. The flour will help thicken the soup.

3. Pour in the broth and toss in the reserved corncobs, potato, and scallops. Raise the heat to high and bring the mixture to a boil, then reduce the heat to medium-low. Simmer the chowder uncovered until the potato chunks are soft when you pierce them with a fork, 15 to 20 minutes.

4. Take the pot off the heat, then remove the cobs from the chowder. When cool enough to handle, use a spatula or spoon to scrape out all the corn milk hiding in the nooks back into the pot before discarding the cobs. This will reinforce the corn flavor.

5. Eyeball half of the chowder and pour it off into a blender. (When blending hot food like this soup, it's always a good idea to crack the lid of the blender to let steam escape and to work in batches, filling the blender no more than half full, to prevent any dangerous hot messes.) Quickly pulse a few times to break down pieces of the potato and the corn kernels. The mixture should be slightly chunky rather than smooth. Pour the mixture back into the pot and add the cream. Stir to combine and heat the cream through.

6. Ladle the chowder into big bowls and garnish with the scallions and cilantro. Serve immediately.

3 tablespoons unsalted butter

1 small yellow onion, finely diced

2 tablespoons minced ginger

2 tablespoons minced garlic

3 ears corn, husks and silk removed, kernels cut from cobs, and cobs reserved

1 tablespoon sugar

1 teaspoon kosher salt

1 teaspoon MSG

½ teaspoon freshly ground white pepper

½ teaspoon freshly ground black pepper

1 tablespoon all-purpose flour

4 cups Cantonese Chicken Broth (page 29) or low-sodium chicken broth

1 medium russet potato, cut into small dice

¼ cup dried scallops

1 cup heavy cream

2 scallions, thinly sliced, to garnish

3 tablespoons chopped fresh cilantro, to garnish

CANTONESE MINESTRONE

SERVES 8

After our son was born, we basically existed off a stockpile of soups my mom and mother-in-law stuffed into every corner of our already jam-packed freezer. My mom made us traditional Chinese soups filled with chunks of black Silkie chicken, whole red jujube dates, and Shaoxing wine meant for optimal postpartum healing. My mother-in-law brought us two coolers absolutely packed with frozen pints of Italian wedding soup loaded with tiny meatballs, matzo ball soup, roasted tomato soup, and minestrone. I was never a soup person before, but the early months of parenthood changed that for me. Now I could never live without at least three different soups stashed away in my freezer for last-minute dinner needs, ready to defrost and devour with a chunk of toasty, buttery bread. This warm, comforting soup is heavily influenced by traditional minestrone, but the base flavors are very Cantonese, starting with the classic holy trinity and the salty, meaty bites of Chinese bacon. It's almost as if our moms joined forces on this soup recipe. Best part is, it's hearty enough to be a full meal, fixing my initial hang-up with vegetably soups that only ever seemed to fuel me for a short while.

Tip
The pasta can soak up all the flavorful brothy liquid, so if you have leftovers to reheat, add a splash or two of water (and maybe another pinch of salt) until you achieve a brothy consistency.

1. Starting in a cold large heavy pot, combine the lap yuk and water. Turn on the heat to medium-high and cook, stirring occasionally, until the bacon begins to brown and crisp up and most of the fat has rendered out and the water in the pot has evaporated, about 10 minutes.

2. Add the oil, followed by the pepper and fennel seeds. Toast the spices in the fat, stirring constantly, until fragrant, about 1 minute. Then add the garlic, scallions, chili, leek, and ginger, and reduce the heat to medium. Sweat the aromatics, stirring often to prevent any browning, until fragrant and soft, about 5 minutes.

3. Slowly add the wine and deglaze the pot, using a spoon to scrape up all the delicious browned bits on the bottom of the pot and stir those flavorful pieces back into the soup.

½ pound lap yuk (cured Chinese bacon) or thick-cut bacon, finely diced

3 tablespoons water

¼ cup olive oil

1 teaspoon freshly ground black pepper

1 teaspoon fennel seeds

6 garlic cloves, thinly sliced

3 scallions, thinly sliced

1 medium Italian long hot green chili or serrano chili, thinly sliced

1 medium leek (white part only), thinly sliced

1-inch piece ginger, julienned

½ cup Shaoxing wine

1 medium russet potato, cut into medium dice

2 cups peeled daikon radish or peeled, quartered white turnips, cut into medium dice

4. Add the potato and daikon, pour in the broth, and bring the mixture to a boil. Reduce the heat to medium-low and simmer for 10 minutes to cook the potatoes and daikon through. They should be fork-tender.

5. Add the celery, cannellini beans, peas, and pasta and continue to simmer until the pasta is cooked through to your liking (you can also follow the package instructions to cook the pasta to al dente). Season the soup with the salt, fish sauce, and MSG.

6. TO SERVE: Ladle the soup into big bowls and garnish with the scallions, cilantro, Parmesan, and lemon zest and juice. Serve immediately.

12 cups Cantonese Chicken Broth (page 29) or low-sodium chicken broth

2 stalks Chinese celery or celery with leaves, cut into medium dice

1 (15-ounce) can cannellini beans, drained and rinsed

1 cup frozen or fresh peas

½ pound ditalini pasta

1 tablespoon kosher salt

1 tablespoon fish sauce

½ tablespoon MSG

TO SERVE

3 scallions, thinly sliced

½ cup chopped fresh cilantro

½ cup grated Parmesan cheese

Grated zest and juice of 1 lemon

VEGETABLES

4
RICE

Chinese people are very superstitious. My mom always said, "Finish your rice, or you'll have an ugly wife." My friends grew up hearing every grain left behind would result in a painful new pimple. Incredibly weird and stressful potential outcomes to come from food waste. But to our moms, these sayings simply meant finish all the food on your plate down to the last little grain of rice. Lick it clean, if you have to. I still do.

A Guide to Cooking Rice	133
And a Bonus Recipe for Restaurant-Quality Day-Old Rice	134
The Perfect Pot of Steamed Rice Without a Rice Cooker	136
And a Bonus Recipe for Crispy Toasted Rice Tea	136
Canned Corn and Scallion Fried Rice	139
BLT Fried Rice	140
Ginger Congee	143
Rotisserie Chicken Congee	144
Congee Arancini	146
Clay Pot Rice (Without a Clay Pot)	150
Roasted Mushroom Lo Mai Fan	152
XO Seafood Lo Mai Fan	154

A GUIDE TO COOKING RICE

I didn't like rice when I was a kid. It was plain. It was boring. It was whatever. And we always had it, every single night. I didn't see the beauty of a simple bowl of rice until I started ruining pots left and right in culinary school when I was tasked with making it for class (very embarrassing for an Asian kid). I had never paid much attention to the Chinese mom trade secrets—the rinsing and the ratios—and it showed. But I'm older (and wiser) now. I appreciate rice. The simple act of rinsing it, watching the water run through the grains. The toasty smell of rice steaming, the scent wafting through the apartment as dinnertime approaches. The versatility. In fact, rice is often the star on our dinner table, especially for my son, who takes massive mounds, balls them up in his chubby fists, and chows down. He is a tiny rice monster, and I promise to teach him all my rice ways one day.

I only call for two types of rice in this book.

LONG-GRAIN JASMINE RICE
This is a Cantonese household's bread and butter. You can use it for your regular old pot of rice, your fried rice, your congee, and your clay pot rice. When cooked properly, the grains fluff nicely on the stovetop and give off a slightly sweet, fragrant scent.

SHORT-GRAIN GLUTINOUS STICKY RICE
As the name states, this is a chewy, sticky rice perfect for steaming. There are a couple ways to prepare it, but my perfect, foolproof method is to soak the rice overnight so the grains absorb as much water as possible and then drain off that liquid and steam. You'll get chewy, individual whole grains of rice, no mush.

RICE

TWO CRUCIAL, NONSKIPPABLE RULES ABOUT COOKING RICE

1. WASH YOUR RICE: Most Chinese moms will tell you a set number of times to rinse. Maybe it's three or maybe it's eight. My mom doesn't count. She simply cups her hand to the edge of the pot as she rinses, catching the grains before they disappear down the kitchen-sink drain. She repeats that process until the water runs nearly clear and free of the dusty starch that coated the rice. If you're not a pro like my mom, I would recommend saving yourself the clogged sink and pop the grains into a fine-mesh strainer, then hold it under running cold water. The ratio of rice to water is super important, especially for fried rice, so I prefer to rinse my rice in a strainer versus rinsing in a bowl. That way, you don't risk losing any grains or holding on to any excess water.

2. DON'T ADD SALT: This is the only time I don't touch salt. Rice is where I draw the line. It's not pasta. It doesn't need to be seasoned from within. A well-cooked pot of good-quality rice has a delicious flavor and texture on its own.

AND A BONUS RECIPE FOR
Restaurant-Quality Day-Old Rice

If you want to go above and beyond and make a pot of rice especially for your fried rice like we do at Bonnie's, rinse 2½ cups jasmine rice in a fine-mesh strainer under running cold water until the water runs clear. To create the driest possible grains for fried rice, the ratio of water to rice is slightly different than for a pot of steamed rice. If you're using a pot, follow the steps for The Perfect Pot of Rice Without a Rice Cooker (page 136), using 2¼ cups water in a medium pot. If you are using a rice cooker, combine the rice and 2¼ cups water in the rice cooker and follow the manufacturer's instructions. While the rice is cooking, line a baking sheet with parchment paper. When the rice is done, dump the grains out onto the prepared baking sheet. Using a fork, gently fluff the rice to break up any clumps and separate the grains a bit, taking care to spread the rice into a thin layer on the baking sheet. Place the baking sheet in the fridge uncovered to chill overnight before using the rice. This makes 5 cups cooked rice (enough for the fried rice recipes in this book).

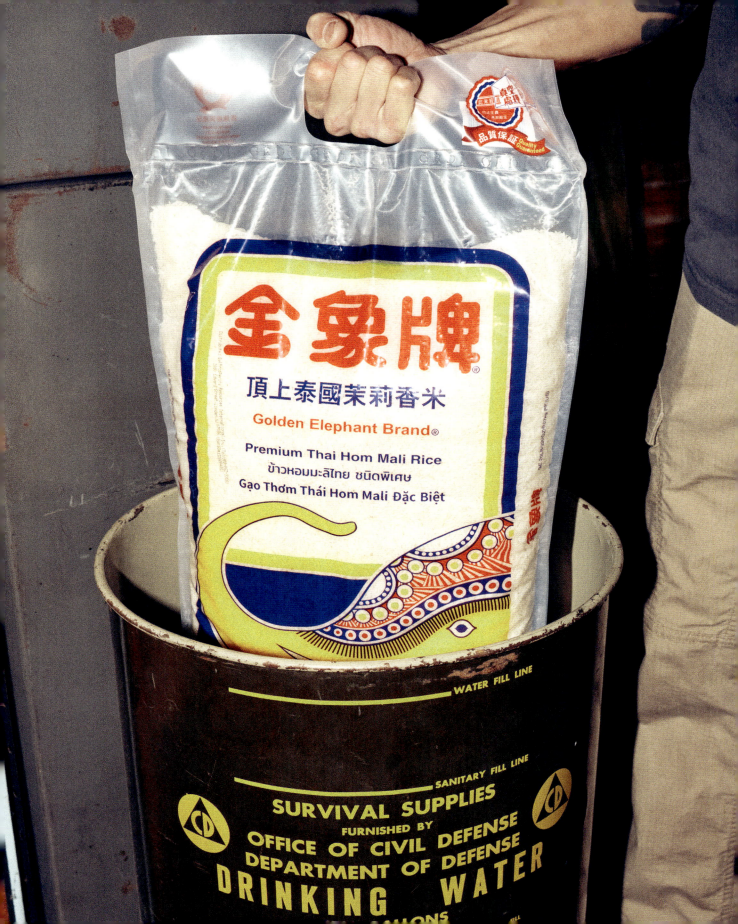

THE PERFECT POT OF STEAMED RICE
Without a Rice Cooker

MAKES 4 CUPS / SERVES 2

I bought my first rice cooker three days before I opened my restaurant. My mom always said that the best rice is made in a pot. She measured her water-to-rice ratio with the lines on her index finger, and her rice turned out light and clump-free every time—no raw bites or mushy bites, no water or scorching at the bottom of a pot. The finger method is a great rough guide for measuring, but if you want to be a little more intentional, I like to follow the ratio of 1 cup water to 1 cup jasmine rice. Most recipes out there tend to have a higher ratio of water to rice, but I've always found that 1 cup to 1 cup consistently yields well-cooked, dry, fluffy individual grains.

1. Rinse the rice in a fine-mesh strainer under cold running water until the water runs clear. Turn off the tap and shake off as much water as possible from the rice.

2. Transfer the rinsed and drained rice to a small pot, add the water, and cover the pot with its lid. Place the pot over high heat and bring to a boil. This should take about 5 minutes. Once the water is boiling, reduce the heat to low and fluff the rice with a rice paddle or the tines of a fork. Re-cover the pot and steam the rice until the grains are fully separated and fluffy, 30 to 35 minutes. Fluff the grains one more time and serve immediately.

1½ cups jasmine rice
1½ cups water

AND A BONUS RECIPE FOR
Crispy Toasted Rice Tea

I crave the crispy, toasty rice bites at the bottom of the pot more than the fluffy rice. Once you scoop all the rice out, you will notice a thin layer of rice stuck to the bottom of the pot. You can gently toast that rice over low heat until golden brown, usually just a few minutes, then scrape it all up. I used to slather those crisp bites with butter and sprinkle them with salt. It was basically popcorn. My mom and grandparents would pour about 1 cup hot water over the stuck-on bits and let the mixture steep for 5 minutes to make a delicious toasted rice tea to enjoy after dinner. A pot with a thick, heavy bottom may not always yield a crust, but the thinner and cheaper your pot, the better the toasty rice bottom you will get. Most people would probably throw it all out, but again, immigrant families don't like to waste anything.

CANNED CORN AND SCALLION FRIED RICE

SERVES 5

You don't need a wok for good fried rice at home. You just need leftover, day-old jasmine rice. That's because the best fried rice starts with fluffy, separated grains. You won't get great results with fresh rice because it still holds on to moisture from the pot, which causes it to clump up in the pan.

Once you have those perfectly cooked grains, fried rice is kind of a choose-your-own-adventure meal. The base recipe is so malleable, you could easily mix and match with whatever you have lying around your fridge or freezer or pantry. Swap out the canned corn in this recipe for 2 cups of anything—think diced cold cuts, frozen peas, chopped romaine, shrimp, tinned dace. There's no limit if you have those beautifully cooked grains ready to go.

1. Heat a 12-inch cast-iron skillet over medium-high heat. Add the butter, corn, and scallions and cook, stirring occasionally, until as much moisture as possible is removed from the corn and the scallions start to soften and take on a little color, 3 to 4 minutes.

2. Add the ginger and garlic and stir and toss constantly to soften the aromatics, about 5 minutes. Transfer the contents of the skillet to a small bowl. Set aside.

3. Wipe the pan clean, return it to medium-high heat, and swirl in the oil. Once the oil is shimmering, pour in the eggs and, using a rubber spatula, scramble quickly until they form big, soft curds, 30 to 40 seconds. Then break the cooked egg up into smaller pieces.

4. Add the rice and toss to warm up the grains, coat in the fat, and mix with the eggs. If the rice begins to clump, use the back of a spoon or spatula to gently separate all the grains.

5. Return the cooked corn mixture to the pan and add the salt, MSG, sugar, black pepper, and white pepper. Toss to distribute the mix-ins evenly throughout the rice, then serve immediately with a pat of butter on top and a few cracks of fresh black pepper.

1½ tablespoons unsalted butter, plus extra for garnish

1 cup drained canned corn

3 scallions, sliced

1 tablespoon minced ginger

3 garlic cloves, minced

1½ tablespoons neutral oil, preferably grapeseed

2 large eggs, beaten

5 cups day-old cooked jasmine rice (see page 136) or Restaurant-Quality Day-Old Rice (page 134)

½ tablespoon kosher salt

½ tablespoon MSG

¼ teaspoon sugar

¼ teaspoon freshly ground black pepper, plus extra for garnish

¼ teaspoon freshly ground white pepper

BLT FRIED RICE

SERVES 6

We have a motto at Bonnie's: Bangers Only. It's a pretty self-explanatory concept. We only make dishes that we know are bangers and we know that guests will love. Fried rice is such a staple dish, and I have high expectations, especially when I'm making it to feed others. That's why I was very hesitant to put a fried rice dish on the menu. More often than not, fried rice is stuffed with far too many veggies and meats and eggy bites, the grains dyed a dark brown from copious amounts of soy. That's not my ideal plate of fried rice. I want bright white grains lightly studded with golden chunks of egg, with a lower ratio of other mix-ins. So once we nailed our rice cookery and landed on that ideal golden ratio, we fried off those perfectly cooked grains in bacon fat, stirred in hunks of juicy tomatoes, and topped it all off with thinly shaved lettuce and globs of Kewpie mayo—a banger that quickly became a staple on the dinner menu.

1. Starting in a cold large cast-iron skillet, combine the bacon and water. Turn on the heat to medium-high and cook, stirring occasionally, until the bacon begins to brown and crisp up and most of the fat has rendered out, about 10 minutes.

2. Add the ginger and garlic to the bacon and reduce the heat to medium. Cook the aromatics in the residual bacon fat, stirring occasionally, until they start to soften and take on a little color, about 5 minutes. Using a slotted spoon, transfer the aromatics and bacon to a small bowl and set aside.

3. Add the neutral oil to the remaining bacon fat and increase the heat to medium-high. Once the oil is shimmering, pour in the eggs and, using a rubber spatula, scramble quickly until they form big, soft curds, 30 to 40 seconds. Then break the cooked egg up into smaller pieces.

4. Add the rice and toss to warm up the grains, coat in the fat, and mix with the eggs. If the rice begins to clump, use the back of a spoon or spatula to gently separate all the grains.

5. Add the cooked bacon and aromatics, scallions, tomatoes, salt, MSG, and sugar and toss to mix and quickly warm the tomatoes.

6. Divide the fried rice among six bowls and top each bowl with a handful of the lettuce and a big dollop of mayonnaise. Serve immediately.

¼ pound thick-cut bacon, cut into small dice

1½ tablespoons water

1-inch piece ginger, minced

3 garlic cloves, minced

1½ tablespoons neutral oil, preferably grapeseed

2 large eggs, beaten

5 cups day-old cooked jasmine rice (see page 136) or Restaurant-Quality Day-Old Rice (page 134)

¼ cup thinly sliced scallions (green tops only)

1 Roma tomato, cut into small dice

½ tablespoon kosher salt

½ tablespoon MSG

¼ teaspoon sugar

¼ head iceberg lettuce, thinly sliced

Kewpie mayonnaise, to serve

GINGER CONGEE

SERVES 4

Congee is my comfort food. At its core, congee is just a bowl of broken-down grains of rice. My mom's biggest tip (which is now my biggest tip) for quickly achieving the ideal delicate, smooth, creamy congee texture every time is to freeze the rice. (Also, don't skip out on rinsing that rice until the water runs clear!) When you take the time to freeze the rice (in a freezer-safe container) for a few hours, it allows the grains to begin breaking down before you even start the cooking process. This drastically cuts down on the cooking time, and I promise you won't have to spend hours at the stovetop constantly whisking. I also promise you'll be shocked at how much you can stretch a single cup of rice to feed a whole family.

The most fun part about congee is that it is a delicious blank canvas, so you can really dress it up however you like. For some, congee is all about simplicity. My mom really likes to add a few pieces of raw squid or slices of fish, slowly poaching the seafood in the cooked grains. But for me, I love all the accoutrements. At Bonnie's, we top our bowls of ginger congee with peanuts, pork floss (a shredded, dried pork product with the texture of cotton candy), fresh scallions and cilantro, a jammy soy egg, and a *yauh ja gwai* (page 98) to serve alongside for dunking. Play with different mix-ins and toppings. Just remember, sometimes less is more.

Note
You can swap in 10 cups Cantonese Chicken Broth (page 29) or store-bought low-sodium broth for the water in this recipe for added flavor and nutrition.

1. MAKE THE GINGER CONGEE: Rinse the rice in a fine-mesh strainer under cold running water until the water runs clear. Turn off the tap, shake off as much water as possible from the rice, and then transfer the rice to a small freezer-safe container. Freeze the rice for at least 5 hours or up to 24 hours.

2. In a large pot, bring the water to a boil over high heat, then gently whisk in the frozen rice. Reduce the heat to medium and whisk every few minutes for 20 minutes. Add the ginger and continue to whisk until all the rice grains have broken down into a porridge-like texture with no whole grains, 15 to 20 minutes longer. Season with salt and MSG to taste.

3. TO SERVE: Ladle the congee into big bowls. Garnish with the scallions, cilantro, pork floss, peanuts, fried shallots, and/or eggs. Set the yauh ja gwai alongside to dunk, if using.

GINGER CONGEE

1 cup jasmine rice

10 cups water (see Note)

2-inch piece ginger, julienned

Kosher salt

MSG

TO SERVE
(choose any or all toppings)

2 scallions, thinly sliced

2 tablespoons chopped fresh cilantro

2 tablespoons pork floss

2 tablespoons roughly chopped roasted unsalted peanuts

2 tablespoons store-bought fried shallots

2 Jammy Marble Tea Eggs (page 82) or soft-boiled eggs, halved

4 yauh ja gwai (page 98), to dunk (optional)

Freshly ground white pepper, to garnish

ROTISSERIE CHICKEN CONGEE

SERVES 4

Every Chinese person loves a deal. That's ultimately why we all love Costco. Every time my family went there to shop, we always snagged a box of croissants (they reheat so well), a large supreme pizza (because it was the same price as a regular cheese), and a hot rotisserie chicken off the spit (because in those days it was practically the same price as an uncooked chicken). We would make that five-dollar chicken last for as many meals as possible. My sister and I would pick the bird clean for breakfast, lunch, and dinner, and then my mom would turn the remains into a pot of congee, throwing the whole carcass in and letting it slowly simmer away with the rice. Once she ditched the bones, we would have the most flavorful pot of congee for the next few days. Honestly, I still dream about that Costco rotisserie chicken. (And I dream of the day I live in an apartment with big enough closets to store Costco-size bulk purchases.)

Note
You can swap in 10 cups Cantonese Chicken Broth (page 29) or store-bought low-sodium broth for the water in this recipe for added flavor and nutrition.

1. MAKE THE ROTISSERIE CHICKEN CONGEE: Rinse the rice in a fine-mesh strainer under cold running water until the water runs clear. Turn off the tap, shake off as much water as possible from the rice, and then transfer the rice to a small freezer-safe container. Freeze the rice for at least 5 hours or up to 24 hours.

2. In a large pot, bring the water to a boil over high heat, then gently whisk in the frozen rice. Reduce the heat to medium and whisk every few minutes for 20 minutes. Add the chicken carcass and the ginger and continue to whisk until all the rice grains have broken down into a porridge-like texture with no whole grains, 15 to 20 minutes longer. As the congee simmers, the meat clinging to the bones will slowly come off cleanly into the congee.

3. Season the congee with salt and MSG to taste and remove the carcass from the pot if you wish. (I enjoy sucking on the bones as I'm eating to extract every last bit of flavor and meat.) Stir in the shredded chicken and warm through, about 2 minutes.

4. TO SERVE: Ladle the congee into big bowls. Top each bowl with the scallions, cilantro, a pinch of pepper, and a drizzle of seasoned soy. Set the *yauh ja gwai* alongside to dunk.

ROTISSERIE CHICKEN CONGEE

1 cup jasmine rice

10 cups water (see Note)

1 rotisserie chicken carcass, 1 cup shredded meat reserved

2-inch piece ginger, julienned

Kosher salt

MSG

TO SERVE

2 scallions, thinly sliced

2 tablespoons chopped fresh cilantro

Freshly ground white pepper

Seasoned Soy Sauce (page 35) or sweet soy sauce (I like Lee Kum Kee brand), to drizzle

4 yauh ja gwai (page 98), to dunk

CONGEE ARANCINI

MAKES ABOUT 12 ARANCINI

A classic New York City slice shop is known for having more than just pizza in its display case. A garlic knot or pepperoni roll, a beef patty, and if you're lucky, a stack of massive arancini stuffed with stringy mozzarella—the tastiest fried bite to dunk into marinara after a slice or two. The base for arancini, risotto, isn't all that different from congee. Luscious bites of rice lovingly stirred on the stovetop becomes the foundation for salty, savory (even cheesy) flavors. So for the base of these arancini, we're making a fresh pot of congee but ditching my usual ratio of rice to water to make a creamy risotto-like concentrate that's much more luxurious and thick compared to the typical loose consistency I strive for. This concentrated congee is easy to load with cheese and country ham before rolling into arancini and frying off to create a crispy, golden-brown exterior enrobing delicate, flavorful rice. These arancini are a little different from the slice-shop version but just as tasty dipped in marinara.

1. PREPARE THE CONGEE CONCENTRATE: In a small pot, bring the water to a boil. While the water comes to a boil, rinse the rice in a fine-mesh strainer under cold running water until the water runs clear. Turn off the tap and shake off as much water as possible from the rice before adding it to the boiling water.

2. Continuously whisk the rice over medium-high heat until the mixture becomes thick and porridge-like, about 10 minutes. Reduce the heat to medium and continue to cook until all the grains have broken down and a thick paste forms. This should take an additional 10 to 15 minutes of continuous whisking. You should have about 2 cups cooked-down rice. Transfer the congee concentrate to a baking sheet or plate and spread into a thin layer to cool down quickly.

3. PREPARE THE ARANCINI: Line a second baking sheet with parchment paper and set it near your work surface. Once the congee concentrate has fully cooled, transfer it to a medium bowl and fold in the mozzarella, ham, Parmesan, scallions, ginger, salt, MSG, and pepper. Using your hands, roll the mixture into balls the size of golf balls and place on the parchment-lined baking sheet. You should have about 12 arancini. Place the baking sheet in the freezer for about 1 hour to firm up the balls.

CONGEE CONCENTRATE

1¾ cups water

5 tablespoons jasmine rice

½ cup shredded low-moisture mozzarella cheese

½ cup finely diced country ham

¼ cup grated Parmesan cheese

3 scallions, thinly sliced

½ tablespoon minced ginger

1 teaspoon kosher salt

½ teaspoon MSG

⅛ teaspoon freshly ground black pepper

4. FRY THE ARANCINI: Pour oil to a depth of at least 2 inches (or halfway up the sides, whichever is shallower) into a small pot and heat over medium-high heat to 325°F. Line a plate with paper towels and set it near the stove.

5. While the oil heats, set up the dredging station. Put the cornstarch into a wide, shallow dish, the beaten eggs into another shallow dish, and mix together the panko and seasoned breadcrumbs in a third shallow dish. One at a time, roll the partially frozen balls in the cornstarch to coat, shaking off the excess. Then dip into the eggs, letting the excess drip off. Finally, coat with the breadcrumb mixture. As each ball is coated, return it to the parchment-lined baking sheet.

6. Working in batches, use a slotted spoon to lower the balls gently into the hot oil one at a time. Be careful not to crowd the pot or the oil temperature will drop. Rotate the balls occasionally to ensure even frying, until they are golden brown all over, about 3 minutes. Using the slotted spoon, transfer the finished arancini to the paper towel–lined plate to absorb any excess oil. Repeat with the remaining balls.

7. TO SERVE: Plate the fried arancini and serve hot with a big squeeze of lemon juice and warmed marinara for dunking.

TO FRY

Neutral oil, preferably grapeseed

⅓ cup cornstarch

2 large eggs, beaten

¼ cup panko breadcrumbs

¼ cup Italian seasoned breadcrumbs

TO SERVE

1 lemon, cut into wedges

1 cup jarred marinara sauce, warmed

CLAY POT RICE
(Without a Clay Pot)

SERVES 2

One of the best clay pot rice places in the city sent you home with the pot they cooked and served the rice in. This massive vessel of food meant to feed one was stuffed to the brim with your choice of protein and vegetable and Chinese charcuterie and a scattering of scallion and a drizzle of soy sauce and do you want an egg too? I loved to dig my spoon straight to the bottom, scraping up those beautiful crispy, crackly bites of golden rice. It was a total steal of a meal. My mom saved every clay pot, but over the years, they slowly cracked and disappeared from the cabinets. So I learned to adapt, making my own clay pot rice with a cast-iron skillet instead, but still serving up the same massive portions.

1. Rinse the rice in a fine-mesh strainer under cold running water until the water runs clear. Transfer the rinsed rice to a medium bowl and add enough cold water just to cover the grains. Set aside to soak for 30 minutes to 1 hour.

2. Drain the rice and transfer to a 12-inch cast-iron skillet. Stir in the 2 cups of cold water, 1 tablespoon of the oil, the salt, and MSG. Spread the rice out in an even layer in the pan and (artfully) shingle the Chinese sausage, bacon, and broccoli on top of the rice in an even layer. Cover the skillet with a tight-fitting lid. If you don't have a lid that fits your pan, wrap a thick kitchen towel around the best-fitting lid, knotting the corners under the handle, to create a tight seal.

3. Bring the rice to a simmer over high heat. This should take about 3 minutes. Then reduce the heat to low and steam for 12 minutes with the lid on. Remove the lid to see if the rice is fluffy and fully cooked. If there is still some moisture or undercooked rice, re-cover the pan and continue cooking over low heat until the rice is done, checking every minute to see if it is ready.

4. Once the rice is cooked, crack the eggs right in the middle of the pan and place the lid back on to steam the eggs until the whites are fully set, about 2 minutes.

2 cups jasmine rice

2 cups cold water

2 tablespoons neutral oil, preferably grapeseed, divided

½ teaspoon kosher salt

¼ teaspoon MSG

2 lap cheong (Chinese sausage links), thinly sliced on the diagonal

¼ pound lap yuk (cured Chinese bacon), thinly sliced

½ pound Chinese broccoli or broccolini, cut into 3-inch pieces

2 large eggs

3 tablespoons Seasoned Soy Sauce (page 35) or sweet soy sauce (I like Lee Kum Kee brand)

2 tablespoons Green Chili Ginger Scallion Sauce (page 31), optional

2 scallions, thinly sliced

5. Remove the lid and drizzle in the remaining 1 tablespoon oil around the edge of the pan. Raise the heat to medium and cook uncovered for 3 to 5 minutes to crisp up and brown the bottom of the rice. The cook on this rice all comes down to trusting your senses. You can't see the bottom of the pan, so you have to rely on your nose (and some key time cues) to make sure the bottom of the rice isn't slowly burning. Perfectly cooked rice should smell vaguely like buttery, sweet, toasty popcorn.

6. Cast-iron skillets retain heat very, very well, so if you don't move quickly, the rice in the pan will continue to cook and brown (and potentially burn), even off the heat. Scrape up the crispy rice from the bottom of the pan, and drizzle the whole pan with the seasoned soy sauce and green chili ginger scallion sauce (if using) and finish with a sprinkle of the scallions. Serve immediately.

ROASTED MUSHROOM LO MAI FAN

SERVES 4 TO 6

There are a couple of different preparations for Cantonese sticky rice. There's a classic dim sum sticky rice dish, *lo mai gai*, loaded with pieces of marinated chicken and mushrooms, wrapped in lotus leaves, and steamed, with the lotus flavor perfuming the rice throughout. Then there's *joong*, the bamboo leaf–wrapped sticky rice laced with Chinese sausage, eggs, and peanuts that is commonly made to celebrate the Dragon Boat Festival. But the everyday sticky rice dish I like to make at home is *lo mai fan*, grains of glutinous rice toasted in a pan and then piled into a steaming tray with any toppings I have on hand and left to steam until each grain is plump and tender and sticky. This roasted mushroom version is an easy weeknight dish—no lotus or bamboo leaves required. All you have to do is soak your rice ahead of time, then it's just a quick steam and dinner is on the table.

1. SOAK THE STICKY RICE: In a large bowl, combine the rice, dried shiitakes, and water. Cover and let soak in the fridge for at least 6 hours or up to overnight.

2. Separate the rehydrated shiitakes from the rice and pat dry. Remove and discard the stems, then coarsely chop the caps and set aside. Drain the soaked rice and discard the soaking liquid. Set the rice aside.

3. Preheat the oven to 350°F.

4. In a large pot, bring a steamer setup (see page 43) to a boil over high heat.

5. PREPARE THE STICKY RICE: Heat the neutral oil in a 12-inch nonstick skillet over medium heat. Once the oil is shimmering, add the scallions, onion, garlic, salted radish, and rehydrated shiitakes and cook, stirring occasionally, until the aromatics start to soften and take on a little color, about 5 minutes.

6. Add the drained rice to the pan and gently toss the grains to coat in the fat, about 2 minutes. Add the oyster sauce, light soy sauce, MSG, and sugar and stir until well incorporated.

STICKY RICE

4 cups glutinous sticky rice

8 dried shiitake mushrooms

5 cups water

2 tablespoons neutral oil, preferably grapeseed

2 scallions, thinly sliced

½ small yellow onion, finely diced

5 garlic cloves, minced

2 tablespoons minced salted radish

½ cup mushroom oyster sauce or oyster sauce

¼ cup light soy sauce

1 teaspoon MSG

½ teaspoon sugar

7. Transfer the sticky rice mixture to a 10- to 12-inch steaming tray. Carefully lower the steaming tray onto the steaming rack. Cover and steam the sticky rice until the grains are tender, fully cooked through, and sticky to the touch, about 45 minutes. Check on the steaming water level halfway through and top off with boiling water if needed.

8. PREPARE THE ROASTED MUSHROOMS: While the sticky rice steams, in a medium bowl, toss the fresh mushrooms with the olive oil, vinegar, garlic, salt, MSG, and pepper, coating evenly, then spread the mushrooms in an even layer on a baking sheet. Roast the mushrooms, tossing them halfway through, until golden brown and tender, about 45 minutes.

9. TO SERVE: Remove the tray from the steamer setup. Top the rice with the roasted mushrooms. Serve immediately.

ROASTED MUSHROOMS

- 1 pound fresh mushrooms, preferably a mix of shiitake and oyster, stemmed and sliced
- ⅓ cup olive oil
- ⅓ cup rice vinegar
- 3 garlic cloves, minced
- ½ teaspoon salt
- ¼ teaspoon MSG
- ¼ teaspoon freshly ground black pepper

XO SEAFOOD LO MAI FAN

SERVES 2 TO 4

There's nothing more impressive than an artfully presented pan of paella: delicately arranged seafood sitting on a bed of rice beautifully colored from saffron and cooked to perfection. Think of this sticky rice as a take on paella. Layers of dried seafood and cured meat build flavor from the very beginning. Fresh shrimp and mussels are nestled into the pan, perfuming the rice as they steam. Plump, chewy grains of sticky rice are coated in soy sauce and oyster sauce and topped with XO sauce. What this sticky-rice variation lacks in *socarrat* (that crispy, crunchy bottom layer of rice in a well-made paella), it makes up for with the quick and passive, foolproof cook and steam.

Note
To devein the shrimp with the shell intact, starting from right behind the head, run a pair of kitchen shears down the shell to the tail, keeping the head, shell, and tail on. Be careful not to snip through the shrimp. The vein should be visible and easy to pluck out.

1. SOAK THE STICKY RICE: In a large bowl, combine the rice, dried shrimp, dried scallops, and water. Cover and let soak in the fridge for at least 6 hours or up to overnight.

2. Drain the soaked rice and seafood and discard the soaking liquid.

3. In a large pot, bring a steamer setup (see page 43) to a boil over high heat.

4. PREPARE THE STICKY RICE: Heat a 12-inch nonstick skillet over medium heat. Add the sausage and oil and cook, stirring occasionally, until the sausage begins to brown and crisp up along the edges and most of the fat has rendered out, 3 to 4 minutes. Add the scallions, shallot, garlic, and ginger and cook, stirring occasionally, until the aromatics start to soften and take on a little color, about 5 minutes.

5. Add the drained rice and seafood to the pan and gently toss the grains to coat in the fat, about 2 minutes. Add the oyster sauce, light soy sauce, MSG, sugar, and pepper and stir until well incorporated.

6. Transfer the sticky rice mixture to a 10- to 12-inch steaming tray. Carefully lower the steaming tray onto the steaming rack. Cover and steam for 30 minutes. The grains of rice should be tender, fully cooked through, and sticky to the touch.

STICKY RICE

2 cups glutinous sticky rice

¼ cup dried shrimp

¼ cup dried scallops

3 cups water

2 lap cheong (Chinese sausage links), finely diced

1 teaspoon neutral oil, preferably grapeseed

2 scallions, thinly sliced

1 small shallot, finely diced

3 garlic cloves, minced

½ teaspoon minced ginger

1 tablespoon oyster sauce

1 tablespoon light soy sauce

½ teaspoon MSG

¼ teaspoon sugar

⅛ teaspoon freshly ground white pepper

SEAFOOD

6 head-on jumbo shrimp in the shell (U12), deveined (see Note)

12 mussels, clams (such as Manila), or cockles, cleaned (and mussels debearded, if using)

TO SERVE

¼ cup XO Sauce (page 37)

Fresh cilantro sprigs, to garnish

7. STEAM THE SEAFOOD: Add the shrimp and mussels to the rice, re-cover the steamer, and steam for an additional 5 to 6 minutes. The shrimp are ready when opaque and curled, and the mussels are ready when they have opened. (Discard any mussels that failed to open.)

8. TO SERVE: Remove the tray from the steamer setup. Spoon the XO sauce over the whole dish, making sure to get sauce on the shrimp and mussels specifically, and garnish with cilantro.

5
NOODLES

A bouncy, springy, fresh-cut rice noodle turns crispy and crunchy in a hot, hot cast-iron skillet. A pack of Hong Kong–style pan-fried egg noodles bake off into crispy wisps and then sog up under a luxurious sauce. A bunch of brittle vermicelli noodles steam into soft strands, ripe for soaking up flavor. A pot of boiled noodles cooked slightly past al dente (perfect for the kiddos) drip in a buttery sauce. The noodle possibilities are truly endless.

Buttery Oyster Sauce Noodles	158
Mac Soup Mac Salad	161
Fuyu Cacio e Pepe Mein	162
Crispy Sheet Pan Fried Noodles	166
Steamed Garlic Prawns over Mung Bean Vermicelli	169
Shrimp and Pork Wonton Soup	170
And a Bonus Recipe for Wontons in a Peanutty Chili Sauce	172
The Rice Roll Ladies on Grand Street	175
XO Cheung Fun	176
Beef Chow Fun	179
Beef Brisket Noodle Soup	182

BUTTERY OYSTER SAUCE NOODLES

SERVES 2

One night when I was a kid, I had a neighborhood friend over for dinner. We were ten years old at the time, and he sat totally still with his hands in his lap for the whole meal, politely declining all the dishes my mom offered him. At the end of the meal, after much insistence from my mom, who couldn't stand to send him home on an empty stomach, he quietly requested a bowl of buttered noodles. My mom had never heard of such a dish. I hadn't either. Her quick-fix pasta was usually a mound of massively overcooked noodles tossed with whatever Chinese condiments we had in the fridge, usually a mash-up of oyster sauce, hoisin sauce, and sesame oil. It was delicious and definitely not nutritious. My sister and I loved it. So these buttery noodles, coated in savory oyster sauce and toasty sesame oil, are dedicated to that friend, to all the kids who don't want to eat anything from this book, and to all the parents (like us) who are too tired to think of anything else.

1. Bring a medium pot of salted water to a boil over high heat. Add the pasta, stir well, and cook according to the package directions. Once the noodles are fully cooked (not al dente), scoop out and reserve ¼ cup of the pasta water, then drain the pasta in a colander and return it to the pot.

2. Off the heat, add the butter and pasta water to the pasta and toss the mixture constantly and confidently until the sauce is emulsified and clings to the noodles (and doesn't just melt to the bottom). If the sauce is too thin, put the pot over medium heat and toss the buttery pasta to reduce some of the liquid. Add the oyster sauce, hoisin sauce, and sesame oil and toss until a creamy sauce forms. Serve immediately.

Kosher salt

½ pound dried pasta of your choice

4 tablespoons (½ stick) unsalted butter, cubed

1½ tablespoons oyster sauce

1 tablespoon hoisin sauce

¾ teaspoon toasted sesame oil

NOODLES

MAC SOUP MAC SALAD

SERVES 8

Mac soup is a *cha chaan teng* staple. Picture big bowls of steaming-hot soup flying out of the kitchen pass, landing on every table in sight. Each one filled to the brim with overcooked elbow macaroni swimming in a silky cream of chicken broth and topped with thin slices of ham or bits of Spam—comforting and familiar and delicious. I love the creamy, velvety soup base, the salty Spam, the overly soft noodles, and the pop of frozen peas. It has always reminded me of a soupy pasta salad, something you'd find at a backyard cookout: a plastic tub filled with noodles and little chunks of meat and perfectly cubed veggies, all clinging together thanks to a healthy amount of mayo. So this is my take on traditional *cha chaan teng* mac soup meets classic cookout pasta salad. The core ingredients are all here in some form, from the chicken bouillon powder to the chunks of Spam to the elbow noodles. Just make sure to really boil those noodles. No al dente pasta allowed in this soup-salad mash-up.

1. In a large bowl, whisk together the mayonnaise, bouillon powder, and pepper. Set aside.

2. In a small pot, bring the water to a boil over high heat. Once the water reaches a rolling boil, gently lower the eggs into the pot and boil for 9 minutes. Remove the eggs from the boiling water and run under cold running water to stop the cooking. When the eggs are cool, peel them and then add to the mayonnaise mixture. Lightly mash the eggs with the back of a fork to get egg chunks similar in size to elbow noodles.

3. Bring a medium pot filled with salted water to a boil over high heat. Add the pasta, and cook according to the package directions. Once the pasta is fully cooked (not al dente), drain in a colander and rinse under cold running water until cool. Set aside.

4. Dice the Spam into pieces about the same size as the egg pieces and the macaroni.

5. Heat a small sauté pan over medium-high heat and then swirl in the a little color and form a crust along the edges, about 3 minutes. Using a slotted spoon, transfer the Spam to a small bowl and set aside to cool.

6. Toss the cooled macaroni, cooled Spam, peas, and scallions in the large bowl with the mayonnaise-egg mixture. Once everything is well coated and mixed, cover and place the mac salad in the fridge to chill for at least 30 minutes or up to 12 hours before serving.

1 cup Kewpie mayonnaise

2 tablespoons chicken bouillon powder

½ teaspoon freshly ground black pepper

4 cups water

3 large eggs, at room temperature

Kosher salt

1 pound elbow macaroni

½ (12-ounce) can low-sodium Spam

1 tablespoon neutral oil, preferably grapeseed

1 cup frozen peas, thawed

3 scallions, thinly sliced

FUYU CACIO E PEPE MEIN

SERVES 6

Right before I opened Bonnie's, I was working at the beloved Taiwanese American restaurant Win Son. One night, I made a fermented bean curd garlic butter to toss with long beans as a special. Rory Campbell, my sous chef, tasted the butter and immediately thought of *cacio e pepe*. I often compare Cantonese food to Italian food. They are both simple but highly technical at the same time—utilizing minimal components and allowing the main ingredients to shine. Both cuisines are also super umami-forward. Think Parmesan, salted fish, anchovies, fermented bean curd. We ran out to buy a box of bucatini, cooked it al dente, threw it into the wok with that *fuyu* garlic compound butter, and served it up for the staff family meal that same evening. Everyone devoured it. The recipe has evolved since that fateful night. Now, at Bonnie's the pasta is garnished with toasted white pepper, a classic note in Cantonese cooking, and grated pecorino to pay respect to the original dish, but the heart of the dish has remained the same.

Tip

If you don't want to make six portions of pasta, you can use the leftover butter as a spread for garlic bread or for a repeat pasta dinner later in the week. The fuyu *compound butter can be made up to 1 week in advance and stored in the fridge or freezer. Remember to allow the butter to temper to room temperature for 3 to 4 hours before cooking to ensure your sauce will easily emulsify. Avoid nuking the butter in the microwave, as you don't want it to melt or the fat and water to separate.*

1. PREPARE THE FUYU COMPOUND BUTTER: In a small sauté pan over medium-high heat, toast the white and black peppercorns for 3 to 4 minutes. You are not looking for color, just fragrance. When you can smell the peppercorns, remove the pan from the heat, pour the peppercorns onto a plate, and let cool. Then, using a spice grinder, mortar and pestle, or even a small blender, grind them to a coarse texture. Set aside ½ teaspoon of the ground pepper mix for garnish. (See Tip.)

2. In a medium bowl, stir together the butter, the ground pepper mix, garlic, Parmesan, MSG, and sugar. Add the drained fuyu cubes and, using a rubber spatula, mix until all the ingredients are fully incorporated.

FUYU COMPOUND BUTTER

1 tablespoon black peppercorns

1 tablespoon white peppercorns

16 tablespoons (2 sticks) unsalted butter, at room temperature

2 tablespoons grated garlic

1 tablespoon grated Parmesan cheese

1 teaspoon MSG

1 teaspoon sugar

1 (300g) jar fuyu (fermented bean curd) in chili, drained and liquid discarded

3. PREPARE THE PASTA: Meanwhile, bring a large pot of water to a rolling boil. Do not salt the water; the sauce contains enough salt from the fuyu. Add the bucatini, stir well, and cook until al dente according to the package directions. It's important that the pasta is al dente because it will continue to cook as you build the creamy sauce. Scoop out and reserve 1 cup of the pasta water and then drain the pasta in a colander.

4. Heat a large Dutch oven or pot with high sides over medium-high heat. Stir in the fuyu compound butter, the drained bucatini, and ½ cup of the reserved pasta water. Using tongs, continuously toss the pasta until a creamy sauce forms. If the pasta is looking dry, add more pasta water in small increments until the sauce begins to look glossy and emulsified but still a little loose. The sauce will continue to tighten and thicken as the pasta cools.

5. Plate the pasta and garnish with pecorino and the reserved ground pepper mix. Serve immediately.

PASTA

1½ pounds bucatini

Shaved pecorino cheese, to garnish

CRISPY SHEET PAN FRIED NOODLES

SERVES 2 OR 3

Traditional Cantonese cuisine is far more rice-centric than noodle crazed. We still have noodle dishes, of course, but a lot of those noodle products are made from milled grains of rice rather than wheat. And while my favorite noodles to eat will always be a chewy, slippery rice noodle, I do have a soft spot for crispy, crackly Hong Kong–style pan-fried egg noodles. The second that sauce hits those thin noodles, they immediately begin to soften, creating crispy-gone-soggy bites that rival the mouthwatering texture of *cheung fun*. Typically, after quickly blanching the thin, yellow egg noodles, you would panfry, or even deep-fry, to get that signature chow mein texture, but I learned this amazing technique from cookbook author Hetty Lui McKinnon that minimizes the mess and makes this a more weeknight-friendly recipe. Simply dunk the noodles in boiling water before a quick flash in a hot oven, and they will crisp up and deepen into golden-brown toastiness. No Dutch oven filled halfway up the sides with oil is needed. As for the toppings, you can use whatever you're in the mood for—chicken, steak, shrimp, or firm tofu paired with any veggies you need to move from your crisper drawer before they wither away.

1. Preheat the oven to 425°F.

2. PREPARE THE NOODLES: Prepare an ice bath in a medium bowl with equal parts ice and water and set it near the stove. Line a large plate with paper towels. Bring a medium pot filled with water to a boil. Blanch the noodles in the boiling water for 1½ minutes. Using a spider, immediately transfer them to the ice bath to stop the cooking. Once the noodles are cold, pull them from the ice bath and lay them out on the paper towel–lined plate. Pat the top of the noodles with a paper towel to remove any excess moisture, then set the noodles aside for 10 minutes to dry.

3. Once the noodles are dry, toss them with the neutral oil, then spread them out on a baking sheet. Bake the noodles undisturbed until crispy and lightly golden brown, about 15 minutes.

NOODLES

¾ pound Hong Kong–style pan-fried egg noodles (sometimes labeled chow mein noodles) or thin instant ramen noodles

3 tablespoons neutral oil, preferably grapeseed

4. PREPARE THE PROTEIN AND VEGETABLES: While the noodles bake, in a medium bowl, whisk together the water, cornstarch, and salt until smooth. Add the protein of your choosing and toss to coat evenly. If you are using tofu, just sprinkle with the 1 teaspoon of salt.

5. Heat a 10-inch nonstick skillet over high heat and swirl in 2 tablespoons of the neutral oil. Once the oil is shimmering, add the protein and cook, stirring occasionally, until it is cooked about 75 percent of the way through, then transfer the protein to a small bowl. The timing will depend on the protein you are using. Swirl in the remaining 1 tablespoon neutral oil, add the ginger and garlic, and sweat, stirring often to prevent any browning, until fragrant and soft, about 1 minute. Add the leafy greens, carrot, and onion and cook, stirring often, until all the vegetables are slightly wilted, about 2 minutes. Remove the protein from the pan.

6. BUILD THE SAUCE: Add the broth, oyster sauce, soy sauce, salt, sugar, MSG, and pepper to the pan and bring the liquid to a boil; this should take about 3 minutes. Return the protein to the pan to finish cooking in the boiling sauce.

7. In a small bowl, make a slurry by whisking together the cornstarch and water until smooth. Pour in the slurry around the edge of the pan and stir into the sauce, mixing well. Bring the sauce back to a boil to thicken, then drizzle in the sesame oil to finish.

8. Pile the noodles onto a serving plate and pour the saucy protein and vegetables over the top. Serve immediately.

PROTEIN AND VEGETABLES

1 teaspoon water

1 teaspoon cornstarch

1 teaspoon kosher salt

6 ounces protein of your choice (such as flank steak, firm tofu, boneless, skinless chicken thighs, or peeled and deveined shrimp), cut into ¼-inch pieces

3 tablespoons neutral oil, preferably grapeseed, divided

1 tablespoon minced ginger

1 tablespoon minced garlic

1 cup chopped leafy vegetable of your choice (such as kale, bok choy, Chinese broccoli, or broccolini), in ½-inch pieces

½ medium carrot, thinly sliced

½ small red onion, thinly sliced

SAUCE

2 cups Cantonese Chicken Broth (page 29) or low-sodium chicken broth

1 tablespoon oyster sauce

1 teaspoon light soy sauce

½ teaspoon kosher salt

½ teaspoon sugar

½ teaspoon MSG

⅛ teaspoon freshly ground white pepper

2 tablespoons cornstarch

2 tablespoons water

1 teaspoon toasted sesame oil

STEAMED GARLIC PRAWNS
over Mung Bean Vermicelli

SERVES 2

One of the beauties of steaming is you can whip up a really tasty, low-effort one-pot meal, like this dish of steamed garlic prawns over vermicelli, in a surprisingly short amount of time. Glass-like mung bean noodles make for a delicious base, absorbing all the best bites in a dish. These noodles are great in a simple stir-fry but are even better steamed under a layer of seafood smothered in garlic, so the bed of slippery, chewy noodles sop up all the sauce. Think of this dish as a play on shrimp scampi: head-on prawns lightly steamed over delicate, springy vermicelli noodles. It's a dish for the buttery garlic lovers, the seafood lovers, and the Rachael Ray *30-Minute Meals* lovers like me.

1. To devein and shell each prawn, using kitchen shears, and starting right behind the head, cut down the back to the tail and remove the body shell, legs, and vein. The goal is to keep the tail shell and the head on (if you kept the head) and to expose just the body. Set the prawns aside.

2. In a medium bowl, soak the vermicelli in warm water to cover until soft, about 10 minutes.

3. In a large pot, bring a steamer setup (see page 43) to a boil over high heat.

4. While the water heats, in a small sauté pan over medium heat, combine the butter, garlic, half of the scallions, the ginger, oyster sauce, soy sauce, sugar, gochugaru, pepper, and MSG. Stir to mix, then heat, stirring occasionally, just until the mixture begins to simmer, 3 to 4 minutes. Remove from the heat.

5. Drain the soaked vermicelli and place in a 10-inch steaming tray. Lay the prepared prawns, backs facing up, on top of the vermicelli. Spoon the buttery garlic sauce into the open backs of the prawns and pour the remainder of the sauce onto the noodles. Carefully lower the steaming tray onto the steaming rack. Cover and steam until the prawns are opaque and firm to the touch, 6 to 7 minutes.

6. Remove the tray from the steamer setup. Garnish the dish with the remaining scallions and with sprigs of cilantro and serve immediately.

10 prawns or large shrimp in the shell (about 14 ounces), with or without the heads

5 ounces dry mung bean vermicelli noodles (about 3 small bundles)

2 tablespoons unsalted butter

6 garlic cloves, finely minced

2 scallions, thinly sliced, divided

1 teaspoon minced ginger

1 tablespoon oyster sauce

2 teaspoons light soy sauce

1 teaspoon sugar

½ teaspoon gochugaru (Korean chili flakes)

⅛ teaspoon freshly ground white pepper

⅛ teaspoon MSG

Fresh cilantro sprigs, to garnish

SHRIMP AND PORK WONTON SOUP

SERVES 8

Very few dishes warm you up from the inside out like a steaming bowl of delicate, plump wontons. Floating in a clear broth, dunked in a peanutty chili sauce, or simply boiled, they are the epitome of a comforting bite (or two). My mom would sit at our kitchen counter, in deep silence, folding wonton after wonton after wonton. Sometimes she'd let me join in, and we would make a few hundred at a time at least—more than enough to give out to my grandparents, eat a few bowls ourselves, and stock the freezer with extras for after-school snacks to tide my sister and me over until dinner. My mom's were (and still are) always prettier than mine, so don't be too hard on yourself if a few of yours come out wonky looking. They'll still be delicious no matter how they look.

Note

You can buy peeled and deveined shrimp at almost any grocery store to cut down on the prep work, but if you do happen to buy shrimp still in the shell, reserve 1 cup of those shells to flavor the broth for this noodle soup instead of using dried shrimp.

1. PREPARE THE FILLING: In a stand mixer fitted with the paddle attachment, combine the shrimp, pork, scallions, water, cornstarch, salt, sugar, oyster sauce, sesame oil, pepper, MSG, and baking soda. Mix on low speed until well blended, then whip on medium speed until a tacky, bouncy mixture forms, about 3 minutes.

2. FOLD THE WONTONS: Line a large baking sheet with parchment paper or plastic wrap. Fill a small bowl with room-temperature water. Set the baking sheet and the bowl near your work surface. Remove the wrappers from the packaging. Work with one wrapper at a time and keep the remaining wrappers covered with a damp kitchen towel to prevent the edges from drying out while you work.

3. Scoop about ½ tablespoon of the filling onto the center of the wonton wrapper. Dip your fingertip into the bowl of water and wet the edges of the wrapper. Fold the wrapper over to enclose the filling, creating a small rectangle. Dab the two bottom corners of the filled wonton with water and bring them together, pressing any air bubbles out and squeezing the corners together to seal. Lay the finished wonton on the prepared baking sheet.

RECIPE AND INGREDIENTS CONTINUE

WONTON FILLING

1 pound shrimp (any size), peeled, deveined, and cut into dime-size pieces (see Note)

1 pound ground pork (preferably 70/30 fat ratio)

1 bunch scallions, thinly sliced

1 tablespoon water

1 tablespoon cornstarch

1 tablespoon kosher salt

1 tablespoon sugar

1 tablespoon oyster sauce

2 teaspoons toasted sesame oil

½ teaspoon freshly ground white pepper

½ teaspoon MSG

⅛ teaspoon baking soda

1 (14-ounce) pack 3-inch square Hong Kong–style wonton wrappers (about 80 wrappers; I like Twin Marquis Square)

4. Repeat with the remaining filling and wrappers and add them to the baking sheet. This filling should be enough for seventy to eighty wontons. If you don't plan to eat all of the wontons right away, freeze the wontons you want to save on a baking sheet until fully frozen, then pop them into a ziplock bag and return them to the freezer for up to a month (and label with the date!).

5. PREPARE THE BROTH: In a small pot, bring the broth to a boil over high heat. Add the dried shrimp, reduce the heat to low, and simmer for 15 minutes. After 15 minutes, all the shrimpy flavor will be released into the broth, so you can discard the dried shrimp or shells.

6. To cook the wontons, fill a large pot with water, bring to a boil over high heat, and add the wontons. (I usually like to serve eight to ten wontons per person.) Boil the wontons until they float to the surface, 8 minutes if fresh and 10 minutes if frozen.

7. Put eight to ten boiled wontons in each serving bowl, ladle the broth over the top, and serve immediately.

BROTH (*serves 2*)

4 cups Cantonese Chicken Broth (page 29) or low-sodium store-bought chicken broth

1 tablespoon dried shrimp, or 1 cup shrimp shells (see Note)

AND A BONUS RECIPE FOR
Wontons in a Peanutty Chili Sauce

Boil eight to ten wontons for each serving as directed, but skip the shrimpy broth. In a small bowl, whisk together 2 garlic cloves, minced; 1 scallion, thinly sliced; 2 tablespoons coarsely chopped fresh cilantro; 2 tablespoons creamy peanut butter; 2 tablespoons light soy sauce; 2 teaspoons black vinegar or rice vinegar; 1 teaspoon Shrimp Chili Oil (page 36) or store-bought chili oil; ½ teaspoon sugar; and 3 tablespoons water until smooth. Drizzle over the boiled wontons and serve immediately.

NOODLES

THE RICE ROLL LADIES ON GRAND STREET

When I was a kid, there were endless rice noodle shops, and even soy milk shops, that all steamed rice noodles for the restaurants in the neighborhood or for customers wandering the blocks. Those kinds of places are sadly fading away, but luckily for me, there's still Kong Kee Food Corp. on Grand Street in the heart of Manhattan's Chinatown. The rice roll ladies there are the sweetest, most helpful women in the business. Every time I walk into the shop, the woman behind the counter will ask me if I've eaten yet. Even if the answer is yes, she still hands me a box of vegetarian *chow fun* with spicy radish and forces a jug of soy milk on me for the car ride home before offering to hand truck my restaurant's massive order of noodles to my car—wherever I'm parked—while constantly scanning the street for the roaming meter maids to make sure I don't get a ticket.

Shops like Kong Kee are why I don't even bother trying to make rice noodles at the restaurant anymore. Trust me, I tried to at one point. I bought all the different types of flour—rice flour, glutinous rice flour, tapioca flour, thin sweet potato flour, thick sweet potato flour, wheat starch, and, one time, even cornstarch. You name it, I probably tried it. I tested with different-size baking sheets and endless steamer setups. Too thick or gloopy or sticky—my noodle rolls were consistently below average, not bouncy and slippery and light like the ones the rice roll ladies steam up. It's not like the recipe is a secret. It's just not the most attainable process for the average restaurant cook, and definitely not for the above-average home cook either. The key is a stone mill, ideally electric, grinding shiny grains of rice and cold water into a fresh rice flour batter, a silky-smooth mixture primed for all varieties of rice noodles—*cheung fun, chee cheung fun, ho fun*, and more. There are countless types of rice noodles on the market, some fresh, some frozen, some dry. Frozen and dry are usually easy to source at your local Asian market, but if you can get your hands on something fresh like the product from Kong Kee, that's always preferable.

XO CHEUNG FUN

SERVES 2

For the last decade, I've been slowly tweaking and perfecting my XO sauce. By the time I opened up Bonnie's, I knew I wanted to showcase it on the menu in a very special way. There are a lot of delicious steamed rice noodles to be eaten in New York City, but very few spots serve a specific style of noodles called *chee cheung fun*. Like *cheung fun* and *ho fun*, the noodles are first steamed in wide, long sheets. But instead of rolling around pieces of shrimp or beef for *cheung fun*, or slicing into noodle strands for *ho fun* soups or stir-fries, the steamed rice sheets are rolled up into a tube-like shape that resembles pig intestines (which is also the literal translation of the Cantonese name for these noodles). Back at the restaurant, we chop those *chee cheung fun* rolls up into smaller-size bites and toss them into the wok with a healthy scoop of XO and a garnish of fresh bean sprouts. The rice rolls crisp up on the exterior while maintaining a soft and chewy center, and the XO packs a big hit of umami.

Note
This style of cooking is similar to a seared gnocchi dish, so if you have trouble finding chee cheung fun, *pick up a bag of fresh or frozen gnocchi or tubular Korean rice cakes. Both options are just as fast and tasty.*

1. Heat the oil in a large cast-iron or carbon steel pan over high heat until wisps of smoke appear. Add the noodles and sear on the underside until a deep golden brown crispy crust forms, 3 to 4 minutes. Then flip the noodles and lightly sear on the second side until a thin crispy crust without any browning forms, 1 to 2 minutes. The goal is to have one side a little crispier, crunchier, and golden brown than the other for a fun textural balance of chewy and crispy.

2. Add the bean sprouts, garlic chives, and XO sauce and toss until everything is well mixed and the chives begin to wilt.

3. Drizzle in the light soy sauce around the edge of the pan and allow the soy to reduce and caramelize a bit before tossing everything together and serving.

2 tablespoons neutral oil, preferably grapeseed

1½ pounds chee cheung fun noodles, chopped into 1½- to 2-inch pieces, fresh (or frozen) gnocchi; or tubular Korean rice cakes (see Note)

1 cup mung bean sprouts

1 cup flat green garlic chives or scallions (green tops only), cut into 2-inch-long batons

5 tablespoons XO Sauce (page 37)

1 tablespoon light soy sauce

BEEF CHOW FUN

SERVES 2

Older Cantonese folks love to judge a restaurant based on its beef *chow fun*. It's a three-part review. The best restaurants' noodles have a slight char; the steak must be thinly sliced, well seasoned, and incredibly tender; and, most important, the price should be fair. But personally, I think this is one of those rare restaurant dishes that tastes better at home. You can tailor the char on your *ho fun* to your liking and slice your steak however thick or thin you like it.

But the real trick here is the velveting, a classic Cantonese cooking technique that tenderizes cuts of meat. You simply whisk together the marinade made with baking soda, which I like to mix with cornstarch, and other classic Cantonese ingredients, like oyster sauce, Shaoxing wine, and freshly ground white pepper. These ingredients will break down the collagen in the meat while flavoring it from the inside out. This technique works wonders on tougher cuts of beef and pork as well as on chicken, creating tender, succulent bites in any meaty stir-fry dish. Restaurants often blanch the velveted proteins in oil or water, but when I'm at home, I don't bother blanching before cooking to save time and avoid a mess. The meat turns out just as silky without it. So now you get to decide on a fair price to charge your family and friends for your hard work in the kitchen. Just remind your guests to give you a five-star review when they leave!

Note
I prefer to cook my ho fun *the same day I purchase it, but if you happen to buy in advance, you can stash it in the fridge for 3 to 4 days before using. The chewy, springy noodles become very brittle in the fridge, and that's totally fine. If you are using noodles pulled straight from the fridge, pour 2 tablespoons water into the pan after adding the noodles to help steam and soften them. That way, they'll have the same texture as same-day* ho fun.

1. PREPARE THE VELVETED BEEF: In a medium bowl, whisk together the oyster sauce, neutral oil, wine, cornstarch, sugar, pepper, and baking soda. Slice the flank steak against the grain and on the diagonal into large flat ¼-inch-thick pieces. Add the steak to the marinade and toss to coat evenly. Cover the bowl and pop it into the fridge for at least 30 minutes or up to 12 hours.

VELVETED BEEF

1 tablespoon oyster sauce

2 teaspoons neutral oil, preferably grapeseed

2 teaspoons Shaoxing wine

2 teaspoons cornstarch

1 teaspoon sugar

½ teaspoon freshly ground white pepper

¼ teaspoon baking soda

½ pound flank steak

RECIPE AND INGREDIENTS CONTINUE

2. PREPARE THE CHOW FUN: Heat a large cast-iron or carbon-steel skillet over high heat. When the pan is just smoking, add 3 tablespoons of the neutral oil. Once the oil is shimmering, add the velveted beef and cook, stirring occasionally, until the beef is browned and cooked about 75 percent of the way through, 2 to 3 minutes. Transfer the beef to a bowl and set aside.

3. Wipe the pan clean with a paper towel if needed, then return the pan to high heat with the remaining 3 tablespoons neutral oil. Wait until wisps of smoke appear, then add the noodles and use a spatula to separate the strands. The pan must be superhot or the noodles will stick.

4. Once the noodles have loosened up, add the garlic chives, bean sprouts, scallions, oyster sauce, and dark soy sauce and toss to mix. Return the beef to the pan to finish cooking and toss continuously until the beef is fully cooked and all of the noodles are uniform in color, about 2 minutes. Drizzle the sesame oil over the top and quickly toss before serving immediately.

CHOW FUN

6 tablespoons neutral oil, preferably grapeseed, divided

1½ pounds fresh or dried ho fun (rice noodle sheets), cut into 1-inch-wide strips (see Note, page 179)

½ cup cut-up flat green garlic chives or scallions (green tops only), in 2-inch-long batons

½ cup mung bean sprouts

1 bunch scallions, cut into 2-inch batons

2 tablespoons oyster sauce

2 tablespoons dark soy sauce

1 teaspoon toasted sesame oil

NOODLES

BEEF BRISKET NOODLE SOUP

SERVES 6 TO 8

There are a multitude of beef noodle soups across Asian cultures. In the States, the most popular (and probably best known) are Vietnamese beef pho and Taiwanese beef noodle soup. Beef, aromatics, noodles, a vegetable or two, an herby garnish—these recipes may have somewhat similar-looking ingredients lists but each component is treated differently to create distinct, mouthwatering bowls of soup. Whenever I'm craving a beef noodle soup, I always gravitate toward the ones with simple, clean, thin broths. Most deeply aromatic beef broth recipes call for you to roast off the bones and aromatics before simmering to add another level of depth. But in typical Cantonese broth recipes, the bones are quickly blanched and then rinsed to remove any impurities before simmering for hours on the stovetop. This results in super-tender brisket and an almost-clear beef broth. It's light and clean but still intensely flavorful.

1. BLANCH THE BONES AND BRISKET: In a 10- to 12-quart pot, combine 5 quarts of the water, the beef shin bones, and the brisket. Bring the water to a boil over high heat. Once the water starts to boil, set a timer for 2 minutes to blanch the bones and brisket briefly. Set a large colander in the sink and drain the bones and brisket into it. Rinse the bones and brisket under cold running water until all the scum is removed. Rinse the pot to remove any scum as well. Put the brisket into a medium bowl, cover, and refrigerate until needed.

2. TO PREPARE THE BROTH: In the same large pot, combine the blanched bones, onion, scallions, kombu, ginger, garlic, fish sauce, wine, salt, sugar, MSG, white peppercorns, black peppercorns, coriander seeds, and star anise. Pour in the remaining 7 quarts water and stir to combine everything. Place the pot on the stovetop and bring the liquid to a boil over high heat. Once the liquid is boiling, reduce the heat to low and simmer the broth uncovered for 4 hours. The broth should reduce by about 25 percent and be extremely rich and flavorful.

3. Scoop out the shin bones with a spider, then strain the broth through a fine-mesh strainer into a clean large pot. Discard the solids. Pick out any stray spices or aromatics before placing the broth back on the stove.

12 quarts water, divided

3 pounds beef shin bones, marrow exposed

2 pounds fatty beef brisket (also called second cut or point cut), cut into 3-inch cubes

1 yellow onion, halved

1 bunch scallions, cut crosswise into thirds

1 sheet kombu

1 (2-inch) piece ginger, sliced

6 garlic cloves, peeled

¼ cup fish sauce

3 tablespoons Shaoxing wine

2 tablespoons kosher salt

2 tablespoons sugar

1 tablespoon MSG

½ teaspoon white peppercorns

½ teaspoon black peppercorns

½ teaspoon coriander seeds

2 star anise

1 pound daikon radish or white turnip, peeled and cut into 1½-inch cubes

4. Add the blanched brisket and the daikon to the broth and bring to a simmer over high heat. Reduce the heat to low and cook uncovered, until the brisket is tender to the point of just falling apart but not disintegrating into the broth, about 1½ hours.

5. TO SERVE: When ready to serve, divide fresh ho fun between six to eight bowls and ladle the broth and brisket over the noodles. The broth will quickly warm up the noodles. Garnish with the scallions and cilantro and serve. If you are using frozen or dry ho fun, boil the noodles in a medium pot according to the package directions before serving.

TO SERVE

2 pounds fresh or dried ho fun (rice noodle sheets) or noodles of your choice

1 bunch scallions, thinly sliced

1 bunch fresh cilantro, roughly chopped

NOODLES

6
MEATS

Dinner at my mom's house was never just the standard carb, protein, vegetable trifecta. It was protein, protein, protein, seafood (also protein), rice, protein, vegetable. There was always meat: pork, chicken, and beef—sometimes only one, sometimes all of the above. Meat would be steamed or wok fried, braised or baked. Occasionally there would be Cantonese charcuterie—*lap cheong* or *lap yuk*—on the side. I usually had a few pieces of jerky for a predinner snack to tide me over before the meal, and there might be an extra serving of steamed pork patty before we cleared our plates. It was a feast of meats every night of the week.

Salt and Pepper Pork Schnitzel
with Chinese Ranch 186

Ham Yue Yook Beng
(Steamed Pork Patty with Salted Fish) 188

And a Bonus Recipe for Ham Yue Yook Beng
Stuffed Cabbage 189

Black Pepper Beef Burgers 192

Sweet Potato Curry Potpie 194

Crispy Chicken Thighs with
Chips and Lemon 198

Steamed Silken Tofu with
Beefy Black Bean Garlic Sauce 201

Mini Sweet-and-Sour Meat Loaves 202

The Roast Meat Shop on the Corner 205

QQ's Poached Chicken 206

And a Bonus Recipe
for the Poaching Liquid 207

Roast Duck (Without a Duck) 210

Pomegranate Molasses Cha Siu 212

SALT AND PEPPER PORK SCHNITZEL
with Chinese Ranch

SERVES 4

I don't really love the idea of batch-prepping meals. I tend to get bored eating the same thing day after day. I do, however, love to make an unnecessarily large batch of lightly breaded, shallow-fried, perfectly golden cutlets to stash in my freezer for those desperate nights I've lost the will to cook. For a crispy texture that holds up after a reheat; I like to use crispy panko breadcrumbs blitzed to a finer crumb. Add in a little peppery kick from Salt and Pepper Seasoning (page 34) during the dredging stage and a quick dusting after the fry, and you've got the perfect cutlet to eat as is or later on. Simply pop the cutlets onto a wire rack set in a baking sheet and slide the pan into a preheated 400°F oven for about 10 minutes to heat through. Your future self will thank you.

1. PREPARE THE CHINESE RANCH: In a small bowl, whisk together the mayonnaise, sour cream, buttermilk, garlic chives, cilantro, lemon zest and juice, mustard, onion powder, pepper, salt, and MSG. Taste and adjust the seasoning if needed, then cover and set aside in the fridge to chill until ready to serve.

2. BREAD THE SCHNITZEL: In a food processor, pulse the panko to fine, even crumbs.

3. In a wide shallow baking dish, whisk together the flour and 1 tablespoon of the salt and pepper seasoning. In another shallow dish, beat the eggs with the oyster sauce until there are no streaks of egg. Pour the blitzed panko into a third shallow dish.

4. Working with one pork chop at a time, dredge in the flour, shaking off the excess; dip into the eggs, letting the excess drip off; and finally, coat in the panko. Using your hands, press the panko layer into the meat to make sure it is evenly coated. Land the breaded pork chops on a baking sheet until ready to fry.

CHINESE RANCH

¼ cup Kewpie mayonnaise

¼ cup sour cream

¼ cup buttermilk

¼ cup thinly sliced flat green garlic chives or scallions (green tops only)

2 tablespoons finely chopped fresh cilantro

Grated zest and juice of ½ large lemon

2 teaspoons Dijon mustard

1 teaspoon onion powder

1 teaspoon freshly ground black pepper

Pinch of kosher salt

Pinch of MSG

5. Line a large plate with paper towels and set it near the stove. Heat the oil in a large cast-iron skillet over medium-high heat. Once the oil is shimmering, working in batches to avoid crowding, add the breaded pork to the pan and shallow fry, turning once, until evenly golden brown on both sides and cooked through, 2 to 3 minutes on each side.

6. Transfer the pork to the paper towel–lined plate and immediately season with some of the remaining 3 tablespoons of salt and pepper seasoning, flipping the schnitzel to coat evenly on both sides. Repeat until all the pork is cooked.

7. Serve with big squeezes of lemon and the Chinese ranch for dunking. If you have leftover cutlets, let them cool completely before wrapping individually in plastic wrap and freezing for up to 1 month.

SCHNITZEL

2½ cups panko breadcrumbs

½ cup all-purpose flour

4 tablespoons Salt and Pepper Seasoning (page 34), divided

2 large eggs

2 tablespoons oyster sauce

4 (¼-pound) boneless pork loin chops, pounded ⅛ inch thick

1 cup neutral oil, preferably grapeseed

1 large lemon, cut into 4 wedges

HAM YUE YOOK BENG
(Steamed Pork Patty with Salted Fish)

SERVES 2 TO 4

The literal English translation of the Cantonese dish *yook beng* is "meat cake." Think of it as a flat, steamed Cantonese meat loaf, a homey sort of dish that's hard to find on restaurant menus. And much like meat loaf, there are a lot of variations of *yook beng* to be eaten. Some households prefer beef instead of pork; some fold in preserved mustard greens or spicy radish instead of salted fish. But the preparation and the steam of the meat patty remain essentially the same. A classic Eng family *ham yue yook beng* is made from a mixture of minced fatty pork, salted and sun-dried *ham yue*, and slivers of ginger. I grew up eating the patty straight from the steaming tray with a bowl of rice on the side, tipping all the unctuous, fatty, salty juices the pork released as it steamed over the fluffy, tender grains and shoveling massive bites into my mouth with a big spoon. This is not going to be the prettiest dish you've ever made, but it's going to be super satisfying, super simple, and superfast—a real ugly-delicious kind of meal.

1. In a medium pot, bring a steamer setup (page 43) to a boil over high heat.

2. Divide the ginger roughly into thirds. Julienne one portion, mince another portion, and slice the final portion into thin coins.

3. Place the ham yue in a 7- to 9-inch steaming tray, layer the coins of ginger over the top, and drizzle with ¼ teaspoon of the neutral oil. Carefully lower the steaming tray onto the steaming rack. Cover and steam the fish to rehydrate until it is soft and pliable, about 7 minutes.

4. Remove the steaming tray from the steamer setup and drain off the residual liquid. Remove the ham yue from the tray, remove all the meat from the bones, and discard the skin, bones, and ginger coins. Mince the fish into small pieces and set aside.

5. In a medium bowl, using your fingers, gently mix together the pork, minced fish, water, cornstarch, light soy sauce, remaining 1 teaspoon neutral oil, sugar, sesame oil, and salt just until evenly blended. Do not overwork the pork or the patty will be too dense.

6. Gently spread the pork patty in an even layer on the bottom of the same 7- to 9-inch steaming tray, trying not to pack it in. Scatter the julienned ginger over the top. Carefully lower the steaming tray onto the steaming rack. Cover and steam the patty until it is firm to the touch and an instant-read thermometer inserted into the center registers 165°F, about 12 minutes.

1 (3-inch) piece ginger

1 (2-inch) piece ham yue (salted preserved fish, about 50g; see page 21)

1¼ teaspoons neutral oil, preferably grapeseed, divided

¾ pound ground pork (preferably 70/30 fat ratio)

1 tablespoon water

1 teaspoon cornstarch

1 teaspoon light soy sauce

½ teaspoon sugar

¼ teaspoon toasted sesame oil

¼ teaspoon kosher salt

TO SERVE

1 scallion, thinly sliced

1 (1-inch) piece ginger, julienned

Steamed jasmine rice (see page 136)

7. TO SERVE: Remove the tray from the steamer setup. Garnish the pork patty with the scallion and minced ginger and serve with the rice.

AND A BONUS RECIPE FOR
Ham Yue Yook Beng Stuffed Cabbage

At the restaurant, we serve up a spin on the classic. Instead of steaming the pork mixture in a thin patty, we shape the mixture into little oblong meatballs and enrobe each one in a napa cabbage leaf blanket before steaming. So now you have it, steamed pork patty with salted fish, two ways. If you grew up with the original, I promise you'll still love the cabbage blankets. If you haven't had either before, you'll hopefully love both versions.

To make the cabbage version, prepare the pork and salted fish mixture through step 5. Divide the mixture into six even portions and form each portion into an oblong meatball. Set aside while you ready the cabbage. Fill a medium pot with water, add 2 tablespoons kosher salt and 1 tablespoon MSG, and bring to a boil over high heat. Prepare an ice bath in a large bowl with 4 cups water and 4 cups ice cubes. Gently remove twelve large leaves from a large head of napa cabbage. Lower the leaves into the boiling water and blanch them until they become soft and pliable, about 1 minute, then transfer the leaves to the ice bath to cool completely. Remove from the ice bath and pat dry with paper towels.

Lay two cabbage leaves vertically and side by side on a work surface, overlapping them by 1 inch and with the stem ends nearest you. Place a meatball in the center of the leaves. Bring the stem ends up, fold the sides into the center, and then roll up the leaves to the end, sealing the meatball inside. Place the cabbage packet seam side down on a plate off to the side. Repeat with the remaining meatballs and leaves.

In a medium pot, bring a steamer setup (see page 43) to a boil over high heat. Place two cabbage rolls at a time in a 7- to 9-inch steaming tray. Carefully lower the steaming tray onto the steaming rack. Cover and steam the cabbage rolls until firm to the touch and an instant-read thermometer inserted into the center of a roll registers 165°F, about 12 minutes. Remove the steamed rolls from the steamer setup and repeat with the remaining cabbage rolls. Serve the cabbage rolls immediately with rice.

MEATS

BLACK PEPPER BEEF BURGERS

SERVES 6

When Phoebe was pregnant, she ordered Shake Shack every week. Everything else tasted terrible to her. So for close to forty weeks straight, every Wednesday she had a cheeseburger, cheese fries, and chocolate shake to celebrate being one week closer to meeting our son. I joined in more often than not—a smash burger is superior to any other style, and Shake Shack always manages to pull off a great crusty char, even for a delivery burger. This is a nod to the roughly forty burgers Phoebe consumed, mashed up with the spicy, peppery sauce traditionally ladled over sizzling black pepper beef, a classic *dai pai dong* (Hong Kong open-air food stall) dish: a simple beef patty smashed in a pan, smothered in a black pepper sauce that caramelizes and crusts around the meat, topped with melty American cheese, finished with raw white onion to cut through all that richness, served on a squishy potato bun.

1. PREPARE THE BLACK PEPPER SAUCE: Heat a small sauté pan over medium heat, then swirl in the oil. Once the oil is shimmering, add the onion and garlic and cook, stirring often, until the aromatics start to soften and take on a little color, about 2 minutes. Add the pepper and toast gently, stirring and scraping often, for 1 minute. Add the dark soy sauce and the hoisin sauce and stir to mix, then add the sugar, MSG, and ¾ cup of the water, raise the heat to high, and bring the mixture to a boil.

2. In a small bowl, make a slurry by whisking together the cornstarch and the remaining 2 teaspoons water until smooth. Pour in the slurry around the edge of the pan and stir into the sauce to thicken. The sauce should be thick enough to coat the back of a spoon. Remove the pan from the heat and set aside until ready to use.

3. PREPARE THE BURGERS: Portion the ground beef into six even balls and set aside.

4. Heat a large cast-iron or carbon-steel skillet over medium-high heat. While the pan heats, slather the cut sides of the potato buns with the mayonnaise. When the pan is hot, working in batches, add the bun halves, mayonnaise side down, and toast until golden brown and warmed through, about 1 minute. Set aside, cut side up, until ready to assemble the burgers.

BLACK PEPPER SAUCE

1 tablespoon neutral oil, preferably grapeseed

¼ medium white onion, finely diced

1 garlic clove, minced

2 teaspoons freshly ground black pepper

2 teaspoons dark soy sauce

2 teaspoons hoisin sauce

¼ teaspoon sugar

¼ teaspoon MSG

¾ cup plus 2 teaspoons water, divided

2 teaspoons cornstarch

5. When all of the buns are toasted, add the oil to the pan over medium-high heat. Once the oil is shimmering, add two beef balls, keeping space between them. Using the back of a metal spatula, smash down and flatten them into patties.

6. Season the smashed patties with salt and pepper and continue cooking until browned and crispy, about 2 minutes. Right before flipping, top each patty with 2 tablespoons of the black pepper sauce, then flip the patties to warm through and caramelize the sauce on the underside, about 2 minutes. Once the patties have been flipped, top each with a slice of cheese and allow the steam to gently melt the cheese. Transfer the cooked patties to a plate and repeat with the remaining patties, black pepper sauce, and cheese.

7. TO ASSEMBLE THE BURGERS: Add one sauced and cheese-topped patty to each toasted bun bottom and top each burger with a few rings of onion. Close with the bun tops and serve immediately.

BURGERS

1½ pounds ground beef (80/20 fat ratio)

6 potato buns, split

2 tablespoons Kewpie mayonnaise

2 tablespoons neutral oil, preferably grapeseed

Kosher salt and freshly ground black pepper

6 slices American cheese

1 medium white onion, thinly sliced into even rings

SWEET POTATO CURRY POTPIE

SERVES 8

A staple spice blend in many households, curry powder snuck its way into Cantonese pantries the same way many ingredients once did: through British colonization. I distinctly remember feasting on my mom's chicken and potato curry almost every other week. A whole chicken she chopped into chopstick-friendly chunks, bone and all. The hunks of russet potato that turned a lovely golden hue from the turmeric in the Madras curry powder my mom tucked away on the top shelf next to her stash of dried Chinese medicinal herbs. A steaming bowl of jasmine rice she served alongside to soak up the lightly spiced curry sauce. That was my mom's recipe, and it was absolutely delicious every time. Of course, I had to go and fuss it up a bit: a buttery, golden potpie crust and a few extra vegetables tossed in for good measure.

1. In a medium bowl, toss the chicken with the cornstarch and oyster sauce, coating evenly. Set aside.

2. In a medium pot, heat 2 tablespoons of the oil over medium heat. Once the oil is shimmering, add the ginger and garlic and sweat the aromatics, stirring often to prevent any browning, until fragrant and soft, about 2 minutes. Sprinkle in the curry powder before the aromatics take on color, then toast and bloom the curry spices in the oil, stirring frequently, until fragrant, about 1 minute.

3. Add the sweet potatoes, broth, salt, sugar, MSG, and pepper and stir everything together, scraping the bottom of the pot with a rubber spatula or wooden spoon to loosen any bits that might have stuck. Raise the heat to medium-high, bring to a simmer, stirring every few minutes to prevent sticking, until the sweet potato pieces are extremely tender, about 10 minutes. Remove the pot from the heat.

4. In a blender, combine the sweet potato mixture, coconut milk, and light soy sauce and blend to a smooth puree. When blending hot food like this puree, it's always a good idea to crack the lid of the blender to let steam escape and to work in batches, filling the blender no more than half full, to prevent any dangerous hot messes. Set the sweet potato puree aside.

5. Preheat the oven to 400°F.

1 pound boneless, skinless chicken thighs, cut into ½-inch pieces

1 teaspoon cornstarch

1 teaspoon oyster sauce

6 tablespoons neutral oil, preferably grapeseed, divided

2 tablespoons minced ginger

5 garlic cloves, minced

2 tablespoons Madras curry powder

1 pound sweet potatoes, peeled and cut into medium dice

2 cups Cantonese Chicken Broth (page 29) or low-sodium chicken broth

1 tablespoon kosher salt

2 teaspoons sugar

1 teaspoon MSG

1 teaspoon freshly ground black pepper

1 (13½-ounce) can unsweetened coconut milk (I like Chaokoh brand)

1 tablespoon light soy sauce

1 yellow onion, cut into medium dice

6. In a 12-inch cast-iron skillet, heat 2 tablespoons of the oil over medium-high heat. Once the oil is shimmering, add the onion and sweat, stirring often to prevent any browning, until fragrant and soft, 4 to 5 minutes. Using a slotted spoon, transfer the onion to a small bowl on the side. Add the remaining 2 tablespoons oil to the pan and the chicken and sear, turning once, until the exterior is crispy brown and the pieces are cooked through, about 2 minutes on each side. Once the chicken is ready, toss the onion back into the pan and stir to mix well.

7. Sprinkle the flour evenly over the chicken mixture and stir to coat the chicken mixture evenly. This will help thicken the potpie filling. Add the wine and deglaze the skillet, using a spoon to scrape up all the delicious browned bits on the bottom of the pan and stir those flavorful pieces back into the curry, then remove the pan from the heat.

8. While the pan is off the heat, fold the sweet potato puree, russet potatoes, and peas into the chicken mixture. Set aside.

9. Line a baking sheet with a piece of parchment paper. Lightly dust a work surface with a bit of flour, then roll out the puff pastry into a rough 14-inch round. It needs to be big enough to fit like a lid over the cast-iron skillet. Transfer the pastry to the prepared baking sheet and lightly brush the top of the pastry with the beaten egg, then poke three small holes in the center of the pastry to vent the steam.

10. Bake the puff pastry for 15 minutes, until the top is shiny and puffed and golden brown. Remove the puff pastry from the oven. Top the potpie with the cooked puff pastry crust and serve immediately.

2 tablespoons all-purpose flour, plus more for dusting

¼ cup Shaoxing wine

1 pound russet potatoes, cut into medium dice

1 cup frozen peas, thawed

1 (8- to 10-ounce) sheet frozen puff pastry, thawed

1 large egg, beaten

CRISPY CHICKEN THIGHS
with Chips and Lemon

SERVES 2

I love a classic Cantonese banquet hall dinner with its massive portions of fried rice and steamed fish and soup and Chinese charcuterie spinning around on a lazy Susan dead center on the table along with its unlimited supply of two-liter bottles of Coke and Sprite. Everyone in my family silently waiting for the star of the meal to arrive, the whole crispy squab chopped into chopstick-grabbable pieces, head and feet included, on a wide platter with big wedges of lemon, ramekins of salt mixed with five-spice powder, white pepper, and MSG for sprinkling, and fistfuls of plain Pringles scattered on top. I've always wondered why we don't top more dishes with chips like that. For a weeknight spin to satisfy that craving for chips over crispy poultry when you can't make it to a banquet hall, I'm relying on the beloved chicken thigh, which is easier to source than a whole squab and is maybe already in your freezer. So here's your excuse to eat chips for dinner any night of the week—with crispy chicken thighs on the side.

1. In a small sauté pan over medium heat, toast 2 teaspoons of the kosher salt, the five-spice powder, pepper, and MSG, tossing often, until fragrant, about 2 minutes. Remove from the heat and pour into a small bowl to cool slightly. Add the sugar and toss to combine. Set aside.

2. Place an oven-safe wire rack in a baking sheet.

3. Use paper towels to pat both sides of each chicken thigh very dry. Use your finger to just barely separate the skin from the meat.

4. Sprinkle the meat side (not the skin side) of the thighs with half of the toasted seasoning mix. Save the remaining half of the seasoning mix to use as a garnish. Lay the thighs, skin side up, on the wire rack in the baking sheet. Sprinkle the remaining 1 teaspoon salt evenly on the skin side of the thighs. This will help to draw out excess moisture. Place the chicken thighs on the baking sheet uncovered in the fridge for at least 6 hours or up to overnight.

3 teaspoons kosher salt, divided

½ teaspoon five-spice powder

¼ teaspoon freshly ground white pepper

¼ teaspoon MSG

⅛ teaspoon sugar

4 bone-in skin-on chicken thighs (about 1 pound)

1 tablespoon neutral oil, preferably grapeseed

2 lemon wedges

12 plain Pringles or shrimp chips

5. About 30 minutes before you plan to cook the chicken, pull the baking sheet from the fridge and place on the counter to allow the chicken to return to room temperature. Pat the chicken skin with a paper towel to remove any moisture that has come to the surface.

6. Preheat the oven to 475°F.

7. In a 10- to 12-inch cast-iron skillet, heat the oil over medium-high heat. Once the oil is shimmering but not smoking, add the chicken thighs skin side down. Move the thighs around as needed and press down using tongs to ensure even browning, about 5 minutes. Once the skin is crispy and golden, reduce the heat to medium, flip the chicken over, and cook on the second side for 5 minutes. This additional 5 minutes will help shorten the time needed for the chicken to finish cooking in the oven.

8. With the chicken still skin side up, transfer the pan to the oven and roast until an instant-read thermometer inserted into the center of a thigh away from bone registers 165°F, about 5 minutes.

9. Remove the chicken from the pan and let rest for 5 minutes. Then serve with the Pringles scattered over the top, lemon wedges for squeezing, and the remaining toasted seasoning mix for sprinkling over the crispy skin.

STEAMED SILKEN TOFU
with Beefy Black Bean Garlic Sauce

SERVES 2

There was a point in developing all the recipes for this book that I reached severe burnout—fatigue, if you will. Utter revulsion for my own cooking and a general lack of interest in making dinner at all. But there was one flavor I still liked after all those months of testing: my Black Bean Garlic Sauce. It's a very malleable, transformative sauce that's good on pretty much anything. It can be used as a condiment to spoon over a silky, savory egg custard (page 122) or steamed fish, tossed with clams in a hot pan (page 227), or simply stir-fried with vegetables. It can even be thinned out with olive oil and rice vinegar to dress leafy greens. So one night as my toddler howled from his high chair, desperate for something other than failed attempts at an unnamed dish that didn't make it into this book, I dipped into my reserve of garlicky black bean sauce tucked away in the back of the fridge. I fried off chunks of ground beef in the sauce and dumped it over a tray of lightly steamed tofu. He devoured it on sight and (not so) politely demanded more.

1. In a medium pot, bring a steamer setup (see page 43) to a boil over high heat.

2. Pop the silken tofu slices onto a shallow 7- to 9-inch steaming tray. Carefully lower the steaming tray onto the steaming rack. Cover and steam the tofu until warmed through, about 6 minutes.

3. While the tofu is steaming, in a small pot, heat the oil over medium-high heat. Once the oil is shimmering, add the beef and cook, stirring every so often and breaking up the meat into small pieces, until browned and cooked through, about 3 minutes. Add the black bean garlic sauce and hoisin sauce and stir to mix. Bring the sauce to a boil, then remove from the heat and set aside.

4. Remove the tray from the steamer setup and gently spoon off as much water as possible from the tofu or blot with paper towels. Don't pour off the liquid off into the kitchen sink, as you risk losing bits of tofu with that method.

5. Spoon the beefy black bean sauce over the steamed tofu and garnish with scallion and cilantro. Serve immediately with the rice.

1 (1-pound) package silken tofu, drained and cut into ½-inch-thick slices

2 tablespoons neutral oil, preferably grapeseed

¼ pound ground beef or pork

6 tablespoons Black Bean Garlic Sauce (page 28)

1 tablespoon hoisin sauce

1 scallion, thinly sliced, to garnish

2 tablespoons chopped fresh cilantro, to garnish

Steamed jasmine rice (see page 136), to serve

MINI SWEET-AND-SOUR MEAT LOAVES

SERVES 4

Americanized Chinese food has made sweet-and-sour a household name. Think glossy fried chunks of chicken, a few sesame seeds, maybe a tiny trunk of broccoli. And while traditional Cantonese sweet-and-sour is made from dried hawthorn berries, a tart medicinal fruit that gives the sour notes to its sweet counterpart in the sauce, sugar, a fun swap is canned lychee. The fruit lends a great balance of sweet and tart with a subtle floral fruitiness. The sticky glaze clings and coats any and all types of meat, especially meat loaf, caramelizing quickly into a light, sweet crust in the oven.

1. PREPARE THE SWEET-AND-SOUR GLAZE: In a small pot over medium heat, whisk together the lychees, ketchup, brown sugar, vinegar, and light soy sauce until the sugar dissolves, then cook, whisking often, until the glaze thickens slightly, about 5 minutes. Set aside to cool until ready to use.

2. Preheat the oven to 350°F. Line a baking sheet with parchment paper.

3. PREPARE THE MINI MEAT LOAVES: Heat the olive oil in a small sauté pan over medium heat. Once the oil is shimmering, add the onion, garlic, ginger, and scallions and sweat the aromatics, stirring often to prevent any browning, until fragrant and soft, about 5 minutes. Transfer the aromatics to a small plate to cool down quickly.

4. In a large bowl, combine the beef, pork, 2 tablespoons of the cooled glaze, the panko, egg, Worcestershire sauce, soy sauce, salt, pepper, MSG, and onion powder. Add the cooled aromatics and gently fold together all the ingredients until mixed without too much mushing.

5. Divide the meat mixture into four even portions. On the prepared baking sheet, form each portion into a tightly packed, uniform rectangular mound measuring roughly 3 by 4 inches. Bake the meat loaves until the tops are evenly browned and an instant-read thermometer inserted into the center of a meat loaf registers 155°F, 35 to 40 minutes. The meat loaves will continue to finish cooking under the broiler.

6. Pull the baking sheet with the meat loaves from the oven. Position a rack in the upper part of the oven and turn the oven to broil. While the broiler heats up, spoon the remaining sweet-and-sour glaze evenly over the tops of the meat loaves, dividing it evenly. Place the baking sheet on the top rack of the oven and broil the meat loaves until the tops are glazed and bubbly, 4 to 5 minutes. Serve immediately.

SWEET-AND-SOUR GLAZE

6 drained canned lychees, finely diced

3 tablespoons ketchup

1½ tablespoons packed dark brown sugar

1 tablespoon rice vinegar

2 teaspoons light soy sauce

MEAT LOAVES

1 tablespoon olive oil

½ small yellow onion, cut into small dice

5 garlic cloves, minced

2 tablespoons minced ginger

2 scallions, thinly sliced

½ pound ground beef (80/20 fat ratio)

½ pound ground pork (preferably 70/30 fat ratio)

¼ cup panko breadcrumbs

1 large egg, beaten

4 teaspoons Worcestershire sauce

1 teaspoon light soy sauce

1 teaspoon kosher salt

½ teaspoon freshly ground black pepper

½ teaspoon MSG

½ teaspoon onion powder

THE ROAST MEAT SHOP ON THE CORNER

"Sikh jó faahn meih aa?"

It's the question my grandma asked my sister and me within seconds of walking through the front door of her apartment every weekend. Literally translated as "Have you eaten rice yet?" the phrase is well known by children of Cantonese parents as a warm welcome, equivalent to "How are you?" If we said no, there was a 90 percent chance she had a plastic take-out container loaded with roast meats over rice tucked away waiting for our arrival, anticipating our hunger—just a light snack from the roast meat shop on the corner.

Roast meat shops are truly the heart and soul of any Chinatown. The glowing windows, warm and bright, filled to the brim with mouthwatering meat hanging for all to see. Platters of chopped poached chicken or roast duck over rice, maybe some cabbage too, rest on well-used countertops. My mom and her mom, like I imagine most moms, never went out of their way to make their own *cha siu* when the roast meat shops in the neighborhood churned out hundreds of pounds of perfect product every day. But not everyone has the luxury of choosing from multiple overflowing meat shops within a two-mile radius of their home, so these are my takes on my three favorite roast meat shop classics, made easy enough to execute at home with little time and effort.

QQ'S POACHED CHICKEN

SERVES 4 TO 6

Bak cheet gai, literally "white-cut chicken" (also known as cold poached chicken), is a super-homey dish. My QQ (the affectionate Cantonese term for uncle) is the *bak cheet gai* pro of the family. He held a chicken-poaching lesson one afternoon at my mom's house, and we were blown away by the simplicity that yields such a perfect chicken, time after time. After a slow and gentle poach in a bath full of aromatics (with the heat off), the chicken chills in the fridge until the collagen sets throughout the bird. The result is glossy, almost slippery (trust me on this), rosy skin enrobing succulent flavorful meat. It is best served cold over a bed of warm rice with a small cup of the poaching liquid warmed up for sipping.

Note

Make sure you are using a heavy-bottomed stainless-steel pot for poaching, such as All-Clad or Le Creuset, with a tight-fitting lid. Otherwise, the pot will not retain enough heat to cook the chicken slowly all the way through.

1. Line a baking sheet with parchment paper. Then take a few minutes to clear out the bottom shelf in your fridge to ensure you can fit a baking sheet with a whole chicken in there.

2. Cure the chicken by generously sprinkling it with the salt, taking care to make sure the salt is all over the surface of the skin as well as in the cavity. Set the chicken, breast side up, on the prepared baking sheet and place uncovered in the fridge to cure for 12 hours.

3. The next day, about an hour before poaching the chicken, pull the baking sheet from the fridge to allow the chicken to come to room temperature.

4. Add 6 quarts of the water to a 9- to 10-quart heavy-bottomed stainless-steel pot with a tight-fitting lid (see Note). Add the ginger, garlic, scallions, and wine, cover the pot, and bring the water to a boil over high heat.

5. Carefully holding the chicken by one leg, dunk the bird into the boiling water. Then dunk the bird in and out of the water two or three more times to ensure the cavity fully fills with water. Gently release the chicken into the water, submerging it. Cover the pot with the lid, and bring the liquid back to a roaring boil. This will happen quickly, so keep an eye on the pot or the final chicken will not be silky.

1 (3- to 4-pound) whole chicken

3 tablespoons kosher salt

6 quarts water

1 (3-inch) piece ginger, sliced

6 garlic cloves, smashed

3 scallions, halved

3 tablespoons Shaoxing wine

2 tablespoons toasted sesame oil

TO SERVE

6 tablespoons Seasoned Soy Sauce (page 35) or sweet soy sauce (I like Lee Kum Kee brand)

6 tablespoons Green Chili Ginger Scallion Sauce (page 31)

Steamed jasmine rice (see page 136)

6. When the water begins to boil, immediately remove the pot from the heat and leave the pot undisturbed with the lid on for 1 hour and 5 minutes.

7. Line the baking sheet with fresh parchment paper. Prepare an ice bath in a large bowl (or a large pot if you don't have a bowl big enough to fit the chicken) with equal parts ice and water.

8. After the chicken has poached for 1 hour and 5 minutes, using a spider or tongs, gently remove the bird from the poaching liquid (don't throw out the liquid; see below). Be extra careful not to tear the skin. Place the chicken in the prepared ice bath for 5 minutes.

9. After 5 minutes, the chicken should be cool enough to handle. Remove it from the ice bath and lay it, breast side up, on the prepared baking sheet. Immediately rub every inch of the chicken skin with the sesame oil. Then place the chicken back into the fridge uncovered to chill for another 12 to 24 hours.

10. TO SERVE: Pull the chicken from the fridge 30 minutes before serving to take the chill off. A tip for poached chicken first-timers: the classic way to eat a whole chicken is to chop it into bite-size pieces on the bone, rather than carve it into individual thigh, breast, and wing cuts. Any red you might see peeking out is just the visible marrow in the exposed bone, so don't stress. Serve the chicken drizzled with the seasoned soy sauce and green chili ginger scallion sauce over a pile of fluffy jasmine rice.

AND A BONUS RECIPE FOR
the Poaching Liquid

Don't throw away that chicken poaching liquid. After you've removed the chicken, lightly season the liquid with a bit of salt and MSG to your desired taste, then strain and serve with chopped cilantro and sliced scallion. You can store it in the fridge for up to 1 week or in the freezer for up to 1 month. Reheat on the stovetop and serve alongside the chicken to sip on. You can also double down on the chicken flavor and use the poaching liquid to poach another chicken for an extra-flavorful bird.

MEATS

ROAST DUCK
(Without a Duck)

SERVES 4

Cantonese roast duck is different from Peking duck. This is not the duck you buy for the shatteringly crispy skin. This is the duck you buy for the flavor under the skin and the marinade stuck to the bones. But this isn't a recipe for duck. It's an ode to that taste of the hoisin and five-spice paste slathered into every part of the bird and of the pan drippings generously ladled over the top of the juicy meat—drippings so good I could almost drink a cup of them on their own. Unlike duck, which can feel intimidating and difficult to source, chicken is unfussy and easy, and a spatchcocked chicken cooks quickly and evenly. So swap out the duck for a chicken and pay homage to those luxurious fatty pan drippings with this roast meat shop–quality dinner any night of the week.

Note
You can always ask the butcher behind the meat counter to spatchcock a chicken for you, and some grocery stores even sell them already broken down. But on the off chance you want to spatchcock the chicken yourself, grab a pair of sharp kitchen shears and a cutting board. Place the whole chicken, breast side down, on the board and, starting at the thigh end, cut along one side of the backbone with the shears. Then repeat on the other side, removing the backbone entirely and saving it for the hoisin jus. Flip the chicken over on the board so the breast side is now facing up and firmly press down on the breastbone with both hands to flatten the chicken.

1. Take a minute to clear out the bottom shelf in your fridge to make sure you can fit a baking sheet with a whole spatchcocked chicken in there.

2. PREPARE THE CHICKEN: In a small bowl, combine the hoisin sauce, oyster sauce, 1 tablespoon of the salt, the pepper, five-spice powder, sugar, MSG, and onion powder and stir to mix well.

3. Using your hands, and starting from the neck area, separate the skin from the breasts and legs. Be gentle to avoid puncturing the skin. Rub the hoisin marinade on the underside of the chicken and underneath the skin on the breasts and legs. Lay the chicken skin side up on a baking sheet. Use a paper towel to wipe off any marinade on the skin and to blot away any moisture. Evenly coat the skin with the remaining ½ tablespoon salt. Place the chicken uncovered in the fridge to marinate for at least 12 hours or up to 24 hours (the skin will dry out in the fridge, which ensures crackly, crispy roasted chicken skin).

CHICKEN

3 tablespoons hoisin sauce

1 tablespoon oyster sauce

1½ tablespoons kosher salt, divided

½ tablespoon freshly ground white pepper

1 teaspoon five-spice powder

½ teaspoon sugar

½ teaspoon MSG

½ teaspoon onion powder

1 (3½- to 4-pound) whole chicken, spatchcocked (see Note), backbone saved and chopped into 1-inch pieces

1 tablespoon olive oil

HOISIN JUS

1 tablespoon olive oil

1 medium carrot, cut into coins

½ small white onion, cut into large dice

1 cup water

½ cup Shaoxing wine

1 tablespoon hoisin sauce

1 tablespoon oyster sauce

⅛ teaspoon five-spice powder

⅛ teaspoon freshly ground white pepper

3 tablespoons unsalted butter, cubed

SALT SUGAR MSG

4. About 30 minutes before you plan to roast the chicken, pull the baking sheet from the fridge and place it on the counter to allow the chicken to return to room temperature. Tuck the wing tips under the bird to prevent burning in the oven.

5. Preheat the oven to 450°F.

6. Using a paper towel, blot the skin side of the chicken to remove any excess moisture. Drizzle the skin with the oil, coating evenly all over to help promote even browning.

7. Roast the chicken until the skin is deep golden brown, about 25 minutes. Rotate the baking sheet back to front and continue roasting until an instant-read thermometer inserted into the thigh joint away from bone registers 150°F, about 20 minutes longer. The chicken will continue to cook (reaching 165°F) after you pull it from the oven to rest before carving. Keep an eye on the bird and tent it with aluminum foil if needed to prevent overbrowning toward the end of cooking.

8. WHILE THE CHICKEN IS COOKING, PREPARE THE HOISIN JUS: In a medium pot, heat the oil over medium-high heat. Once the oil is shimmering, add the chicken back pieces and brown on all sides, 4 to 5 minutes total. Add the carrot and onion and cook, stirring often, until the vegetables start to soften and take on a little color, 4 to 5 minutes. Add the water and wine and deglaze the pot, using a spoon to scrape up all the delicious browned bits on the bottom of the pot and stir those flavorful pieces back into the jus. Bring the jus to a boil, then reduce the heat to medium-low and simmer until reduced by half, 25 to 30 minutes.

9. Strain the jus through a fine-mesh strainer into a small heatproof bowl, discarding the bones, onion, and carrot. Then return the jus to the pot off the heat and whisk in the hoisin sauce, oyster sauce, five-spice powder, and pepper until fully combined. Still off the heat, whisk in the butter, one cube at a time, until the sauce is fully emulsified and thickened.

10. TO SERVE: After pulling the chicken from the oven, leave it on the baking sheet to rest for 10 minutes before carving and serving with the hoisin jus.

POMEGRANATE MOLASSES CHA SIU

SERVES 4 TO 6

Good *cha siu* can be hard to find and even harder to replicate at home. The pork should be the right balance of sweet and salty, fatty and lean—a touch sticky, and with just the right amount of char on the crust. The secret is all in the cook. Classic roast meat shops hang strips of pork in a vertical oven built specifically for roasting meats that blasts the meat evenly with heat while the cooks frequently baste the strips with a sticky glaze. To mimic that action at home, the pork is elevated on a wire rack to get maximum airflow and then basted and flipped and flipped and basted in the oven. This is a relatively traditional marinade (minus any red yeast rice or red food dye for that signature *cha siu* red ring) with a tiny twist: pomegranate molasses. I like to lean on fruits in my *cha siu* marinade, sometimes blitzing cherries or strawberries into the mix, but pomegranate molasses is a wonderful, sticky-sweet addition that yields a gorgeous glossy, glazed crust.

Note

When you order cha siu, *you can often request fatty, half fatty, or lean from the person chopping the meat behind the counter, referring to the fat content of the pork. If you prefer fattier* cha siu, *use pork belly for this recipe. It's not the traditional cut, but it gives you that same unctuous mouthfeel. If you prefer a leaner* cha siu, *opt for the more traditional cut, the pork collar, which is sometimes labeled as coppa (not to be confused with the Italian charcuterie) in butcher shops. You don't want something too lean, like a pork tenderloin, which would just dry out in the oven, turning tough and unpleasant.*

1. PREPARE THE MARINADE: In a medium bowl, whisk together the garlic, sugar, 2 tablespoons of the pomegranate molasses, the light soy sauce, hoisin sauce, wine, 2 teaspoons of the honey, the salt, MSG, five-spice powder, and sesame oil, mixing well. Reserve ¼ cup of the marinade for the glaze and set aside in the fridge.

MARINADE

6 garlic cloves, grated

¼ cup sugar

4 tablespoons pomegranate molasses, divided

2 tablespoons light soy sauce

1½ tablespoons hoisin sauce

2 teaspoons Shaoxing wine

6 teaspoons honey, divided

2 teaspoons kosher salt

½ teaspoon MSG

½ teaspoon five-spice powder

½ teaspoon toasted sesame oil

RECIPE AND INGREDIENTS CONTINUE

2. PREP THE PORK: If you are using pork belly, divide the slab into four roughly even quadrants. If you are using pork collar, lay the meat on a cutting board and use a chef's knife to cut parallel to the board, slicing through the length of the meat from one side almost all the way to the other side, until you can open the collar up like a book, creating a roughly 1- to 1½-inch-thick piece. Drop the pork along with the marinade into a ziplock bag. Press the air out of the bag, seal, and massage the marinade into the pork. Pop the bag into the fridge to marinate the pork for at least 12 hours or up to 24 hours.

3. Preheat the oven to 475°F. Line a rimmed baking sheet with aluminum foil (this will help with cleanup) and set a wire rack in the baking sheet.

4. While the oven preheats, remove the pork from the bag and place it on the prepared rack.

5. In a small bowl, whisk together the reserved ¼ cup marinade, the remaining 2 tablespoons pomegranate molasses, and the remaining 4 teaspoons honey to create a glaze.

6. Add the water to the baking sheet to prevent the drippings from burning or smoking and place the pork in the oven to roast for 10 minutes. Then reduce the oven temperature to 400°F and continue to roast for another 10 minutes.

7. Remove the pork from the oven. Using tongs, flip the pork and rotate it on the baking sheet, then return the pan to the oven and continue to roast until the pork is nearly cooked through, about 10 minutes.

8. Remove the pork from the oven again and baste the top of the pork with roughly one-third of the pomegranate molasses glaze.

9. Position a rack in the upper part of the oven and turn the oven to broil.

10. Pop the glazed pork onto the top rack of the oven and broil to caramelize the sugars in the glaze, creating charred bits, about 3 minutes. Remove the pork from the oven, flip it again, and baste the top with half of the remaining pomegranate molasses glaze. Broil to caramelize the sugars in the glaze, creating charred bits, about 3 minutes.

11. Remove the pork from the oven, transfer to a cutting board, and let rest for 10 minutes before cutting into ⅛-inch-thick slices. Brush the remaining glaze over the top of the sliced pork, then serve with hot mustard (if using).

PORK

1 (2-pound) skinless pork belly slab
   or pork collar (see Note)

2 cups water

Chinese Hot Mustard (page 30),
   to serve (optional)

MEATS

7
SEAFOOD

You can judge how good a Cantonese restaurant or supermarket's seafood selection is by the size of its fish tank. The old folks covet freshly caught seafood, so much so that my grandpa flat out refused to eat fish that he didn't see swimming in a tank that same morning. Tanks filled with crabs, lobsters, and fish, all stacked on top of one another, fill the front entrances of the best spots in Chinatown. Shrimp and clams and mussels spill out onto display cases lined with sparkling ice. Look for bright, clear eyes and firm flesh in whole fish and for lobsters that are moving and grooving. Be confident and point out which shellfish or fish you want. Now is not the time to be shy.

Sizzling Steamed Fish
with Seasoned Soy Sauce 218

FFLT (Fried Fish, Lettuce, Tomato)
Sandwich 221

Grilled Squid Salad
with Preserved Lemon 222

Clams Casino 224

Clams with Black Bean Garlic Sauce 227

Hup To Ha (Shrimp and Walnuts) 228

Lobster Cantonese 232

SIZZLING STEAMED FISH
with Seasoned Soy Sauce

SERVES 2

If a roast chicken is the quintessential American home-cooked meal, a steamed fish is its Cantonese counterpart. Delicate flesh, lightly sweet, never any leftovers—it hits all the marks. My mom taught me to make tiny slits along the flesh of the fish, big enough to slide coins of ginger into, so the ginger perfumes the fish from the inside out as the fish quickly steams.

Tip
This technique also works great for fish fillets. Lay the thin ginger slices on top of two 6- to 8-ounce fish fillets in a steaming tray, then bring a steamer setup to a boil over high heat. Follow the directions from step 4 onward, steaming the fish fillets for about 7 minutes.

1 (2-inch) piece ginger

1 (1½- to 2-pound) whole fish (I like sea bass), scaled and gutted (ask the fishmonger to do this for you to avoid the mess at home)

¼ cup plus 1 teaspoon neutral oil, preferably grapeseed, divided

1 tablespoon light soy sauce

1 tablespoon Seasoned Soy Sauce or sweet soy sauce (I like Lee Kum Kee brand) (page 35)

2 scallions, finely julienned

Fresh cilantro sprigs, to garnish

Steamed jasmine rice (see page 136), to serve

1. Divide the piece of ginger in half crosswise. Finely julienne one 1-inch piece and thinly slice the other 1-inch piece.

2. In a large pot, bring a steamer setup (see page 43) to a boil over high heat.

3. Use a sharp knife to cut three shallow, diagonal slits on one side of the fish, spacing them about 2 inches apart and cutting almost down to the bone. Insert the sliced ginger into the slits.

4. Brush 1 teaspoon of the oil over a 10- to 12-inch steaming tray to prevent sticking. Place the fish in the prepared steaming tray and carefully lower the tray onto the steaming rack. Cover and steam the fish until the flesh and eyes are opaque, 12 to 14 minutes.

5. Remove the tray from the steamer setup and drain off any liquid that has accumulated into the kitchen sink or a small bowl. Discard the ginger slices in the fish. Transfer the fish to a platter, or you can leave it in the steaming tray to serve as my mom does. Drizzle the light soy sauce and seasoned soy sauce over the fish, then scatter the julienned ginger and scallion on top.

6. In a small sauté pan over high heat, heat the remaining ¼ cup oil until gentle wisps of smoke appear. Gently pour the hot oil over the ginger and scallion to cook the aromatics and caramelize the soy sauces. Garnish with cilantro sprigs and serve with the rice on the side.

FFLT (FRIED FISH, LETTUCE, TOMATO) SANDWICH

SERVES 4

Admittedly, I never thought twice about those Chinese bakery fried fish sandwiches. Seafood on the display shelf in a bakery never really called my name, but one day, I randomly opted for the fish, and I've never looked back. Fresh, squishy milk bread buns sandwiching just fried fish, a bit of shredded lettuce, and a slice of tomato—it's so simple and so good. The only change-up here is swapping the more traditional flour, egg, panko trifecta for a wet beer batter that comes together quickly. While wet batters may be messier, they yield a far superior light and crispy, airy crust—the perfect coating for a fried fish sando.

1. PREPARE THE FISH: In a small bowl, mix together 2 tablespoons of the salt and the sugar. Sprinkle evenly over the fish fillets and leave the fillets to cure at room temperature for 20 minutes. Rinse the fillets and pat dry with paper towels.

2. FRY THE FISH: Pour oil to a depth of at least 2 inches (or halfway up the sides, whichever is shallower) into a large pot or Dutch oven and heat over medium-high heat to 375°F. Line a plate with paper towels and set it near the stove.

3. PREPARE THE BEER BATTER: Evenly sprinkle ¼ cup of the cornstarch on a large flat plate. In a medium bowl, whisk together the remaining ½ cup cornstarch, the flour, the remaining 1 teaspoon salt, the MSG, Old Bay Seasoning, pepper, and baking powder. Slowly stream in the beer, whisking constantly until a smooth batter forms. One at a time, dredge the fish pieces in the cornstarch, coating both sides and shaking off the excess, and then dunk them into the batter, coating fully and letting the excess drip off. Set aside on a plate.

4. When the oil is ready, one at a time, gently lower each piece of fish into the oil and deep-fry, flipping halfway through, until the batter is golden brown and the fish is cooked through, 5 to 6 minutes. Using tongs, transfer the fried fish to the paper towel–lined plate.

5. TO ASSEMBLE THE SANDWICH: Smear a thin layer of mayonnaise on the cut sides of the buns, saving some for later. Heat a large sauté pan over medium heat. When the pan is hot, working in batches, add the bun halves, mayonnaise side down, and toast until golden brown and warmed through, about 1 minute. Slather more mayonnaise on the cut sides of the buns, then layer a fried fish fillet on each bun bottom, followed by one-fourth of the lettuce and a tomato slice. Season the tomato slices with salt and pepper, then close with the bun tops. Serve immediately with big squeezes of lemon.

FISH

2 tablespoons plus 1 teaspoon kosher salt, divided

1 tablespoon sugar

4 (¼-pound) haddock, hake, or cod fillets

Neutral oil, preferably grapeseed, for frying

¾ cup cornstarch, divided

¼ cup all-purpose flour

1 teaspoon MSG

1 teaspoon Old Bay Seasoning

½ teaspoon freshly ground black pepper

½ teaspoon baking powder

¾ cup light lager beer

SANDWICH

6 tablespoons Kewpie mayonnaise or Ginger-Scallion Tartar Sauce (page 88)

4 milk bread buns (page 60) or soft, pillowy potato buns

2 cups shredded iceberg lettuce

4 large slices heirloom tomato

Kosher salt and freshly ground black pepper

4 lemon wedges, to serve

GRILLED SQUID SALAD
with Preserved Lemon

SERVES 6

My restaurant is in a super-Italian-heavy part of the neighborhood, and we're blessed with amazing bakeries, pasta makers, sandwich shops, and delis all within a five-minute walk. Right up the block is one of my favorite pork stores, which has a packed cold case filled with prosciutto, marinated peppers, mozzarella, sausages, and pasta salad. We all love to snag a sandwich from that shop, but one day my sous chef walked in with a deli cup container of the marinated squid salad from the cold case. It was bright and acidic, something Cantonese food usually isn't, but the flavors still felt super familiar. So we riffed on it. We swapped the red wine vinegar for rice vinegar and the parsley for scallion and cilantro, then added pickled mustard greens to the briny olives. And thus, the Cantonese marinated grilled squid salad was made a special on the menu—a hit in the hot, steamy, sweaty summer months.

Note
Squid size can vary greatly. If you have larger pieces of squid, break them down to roughly 4- to 5-inch sections to prevent overcooking.

1. Fill a medium bowl with water, add the mustard greens, and let soak for 30 minutes. Drain the mustard greens and discard the soaking liquid. Wrap the greens in a paper towel and squeeze out any residual water. Set aside.

2. Heat a grill to high or a grill pan over high heat. Brush the grill with the neutral oil. When the grill is hot, cook the squid, turning once, until lightly charred and cooked through, about 2 minutes on each side. Transfer to a plate and let cool completely.

3. While the squid is cooling, prepare the marinade. In a large bowl, combine the mustard greens, celery, onion, olives, preserved lemon rind, vinegar, lemon juice, olive oil, garlic, salt, pepper, and MSG. Toss to coat everything fully.

4. When the squid is cool, slice the tubes into ¼-inch-wide rings and cut any large tentacles in half. Add the squid to the large bowl, give a good toss to coat evenly with the marinade, and then cover and place in the fridge to marinate for 6 hours.

5. Right before serving, toss in the cilantro and scallions.

1 cup drained and coarsely chopped pickled mustard greens

3 tablespoons neutral oil, preferably grapeseed

1 pound cleaned squid, tubes and tentacles (see Note)

1 celery stalk, thinly sliced

½ small red onion, thinly sliced

12 Castelvetrano olives, pitted and halved

1 whole preserved lemon rind (no flesh), finely minced

3 tablespoons rice vinegar

3 tablespoons freshly squeezed lemon juice

3 tablespoons olive oil

1 garlic clove, minced

1 teaspoon kosher salt

¼ teaspoon freshly ground black pepper

¼ teaspoon MSG

¼ cup chopped fresh cilantro

2 scallions, thinly sliced

CLAMS CASINO

SERVES 4

These clams bring me back to my college internship days at a Long Island country club. I would drive more than an hour every day in the summer heat to make salads and sneakily eat the clams casino the kitchen served. There was only one person allowed to make those clams, and if he was out that day, we didn't serve them. They were phenomenal. Big, buttery seasoned breadcrumbs, plump clam bellies—I can't tell you anything else about them (he wouldn't share the recipe), but just know that they were perfect. So the base of these clams is a take on his version from what I can remember, plus fatty bites of Chinese sausage, Shaoxing wine, and fermented black soybeans to make it a little more me.

1. PURGE THE CLAMS: Place the clams in a medium bowl in the sink and run cold water over them continuously to clean off as much sand as possible from the outside. Once the water is clear, fill the bowl with fresh water and place the bowl in the fridge for 1 hour to purge all the sand and grit from inside the clams. Remove the clams from the fridge and rinse again to remove any remaining sand.

2. PREPARE THE BREADCRUMBS: In a small sauté pan over medium heat, cook the sausage, stirring occasionally, until it begins to brown and crisp up along the edges and most of the fat has rendered out, about 3 minutes. Swirl in the neutral oil, then add the breadcrumbs, salt, pepper, and MSG and lightly toast the crumbs, stirring often. Once they take on a little color, after about 2 minutes, remove the pan from the heat and scrape the crumbs into a small bowl.

3. PREPARE THE CLAM STUFFING: Heat the olive oil in a medium pot over medium heat. Add the sausage and cook, stirring occasionally, until it begins to brown and crisp up along the edges and most of the fat has rendered out, about 3 minutes. Add the shallots, garlic, scallion, fermented black soybeans, and cilantro and slowly caramelize in the fat, stirring occasionally, until the aromatics start to soften and take on color, about 5 minutes. Add the wine and water and deglaze the pot, using a spoon to scrape up all the delicious browned bits on the bottom of the pot and stir those flavorful pieces back into the clam stuffing.

4. Add the cleaned clams to the pot and quickly cover with a tight-fitting lid to steam them open. Crank up the heat to high. It should take 2 to 4 minutes (depending on the size of the clams) for the majority to open. Remove all the clams that have opened to a large bowl and place the lid back on the pot, giving the remaining clams another 2 minutes to open. Pull the remaining opened clams from the pot. If some clams do not open, discard them because they are probably not safe to eat.

36 Manila clams (about 4 pounds)

BREADCRUMBS

1 lap cheong (Chinese sausage link), cut into small dice

1 teaspoon neutral oil, preferably grapeseed

1 cup panko breadcrumbs

¼ teaspoon kosher salt

¼ teaspoon freshly ground white pepper

¼ teaspoon MSG

Continue cooking the liquid in the pot over high heat without the lid, stirring often, until a jammy paste forms, 3 to 4 minutes. Using a spoon or rubber spatula, scrape the jammy paste into a small heatproof bowl and set aside to cool to room temperature.

5. Carefully pry off the top shell from each open clam and discard. Double-check that there are no shell fragments in the bottom shells, then arrange the clams in their shells in a single layer in a large baking dish.

6. Once the jammy paste has cooled, add the butter to it and, using a rubber spatula, mix together the paste and butter to make the filling. Scoop a generous teaspoon of the filling atop each clam, then generously sprinkle the breadcrumb mixture evenly over the top.

7. You want to eat these piping hot, right from the oven, so if you plan to serve them later, pop them into the fridge at this stage. When you're ready to serve, preheat the oven to 450°F.

8. Bake the clams until the breadcrumbs turn golden brown, 5 to 6 minutes. As soon as you pull the clams from the oven, hit them with freshly grated lemon zest. Cut the lemon into wedges and add a big squeeze of juice right before serving immediately.

CLAM STUFFING

1 tablespoon olive oil

1 lap cheong (Chinese sausage link), cut into small dice

2 medium shallots, minced

2 tablespoons minced garlic

1 scallion, thinly sliced

1 tablespoon minced fermented black soybeans

1 tablespoon chopped fresh cilantro

3 tablespoons Shaoxing wine

3 tablespoons water

½ cup (1 stick) unsalted butter, at room temperature

1 lemon

SEAFOOD

CLAMS
with Black Bean Garlic Sauce

SERVES 2 TO 4

Clams with black bean garlic sauce is a dish that's just about as classic as they come—a Cantonese restaurant mainstay. The average restaurant makes the black bean garlic sauce to order superfast in a ripping-hot wok, quickly spooning in all the ingredients with lightning speed while the clams lightly steam open in the saucy aromatics. I prefer to make this sauce separately for two reasons. Number one, you run the risk of overcooked, rubbery, chewy clams or burnt sauce. I'm a fast cook, but I'm not as fast as the seasoned pros, and even my clams would be past their prime. Number two, this garlicky black bean sauce is meant to be eaten over anything and everything. So make a double batch, pop the unused half into the fridge, and make Steamed Silken Tofu with Beefy Black Bean Garlic Sauce (page 201) later in the week.

1. Place the clams in a medium bowl in the sink and run cold water over them to clean off as much sand as possible from the outside. Once the water is clear, cover the clams with fresh water and place the bowl in the fridge for 1 hour to purge all the sand and grit from inside the clams. Remove the clams from the fridge and rinse again to remove any remaining sand.

2. Heat a large cast-iron or carbon-steel skillet or a large wok over medium-high heat, then swirl in the oil. Once the oil is shimmering, add the chili, onion, and garlic and cook, stirring occasionally, until the aromatics start to soften and take on a little color, about 30 seconds.

3. Add the clams and toss with the aromatics. Cover with a lid and cook until most of the clams have started to open, 2 to 3 minutes. If you're using littlenecks, they may take closer to 5 to 6 minutes to open.

4. Add the black bean sauce and toss the clams quickly to coat, then bring the sauce to a boil to finish cooking them. All the clams should open. If one or two don't, toss them because they are probably not safe to eat.

5. Transfer the clams to a platter and garnish with cilantro sprigs. Serve with the rice on the side.

2 pounds Manila or littleneck clams or cockles

2 tablespoons neutral oil, preferably grapeseed

1 Italian long hot green chili or serrano chili, seeded and sliced into thin rings

½ medium red onion, cut into medium dice

2 garlic cloves, minced

1½ cups Black Bean Garlic Sauce (page 28)

Fresh cilantro sprigs, to garnish

Steamed jasmine rice (see page 136), to serve

HUP TO HA
(Shrimp and Walnuts)

SERVES 4

Before our son was born, there were only two things we knew for certain. Number one, we were going to throw him a party to celebrate his first one hundred days in our arms at a Chinese banquet hall deep in Brooklyn. And number two, whatever venue we booked had to serve overflowing platters of *hup to ha* to all our loved ones. A Cantonese classic, *hup to ha* is a near-perfect dish: fried shrimp thickly coated in a sauce made from Kewpie mayonnaise sweetened with condensed milk and honey, shatteringly crispy candied walnuts dotted with toasted white sesame seeds, wheels of juicy orange, and quickly blanched broccoli. When I make this dish at home, I don't change a thing other than seasoning the broccoli just a touch with kosher salt and MSG. The rest of parenting is up in the air, but at least we know we can throw a great banquet party for a three-month-old.

Note
This is a fussier dish because it requires a lot of oil. I swear I tried to simplify this, but for the best results, you cannot reuse the oil you fry the sugary walnuts in. So you will need to discard that oil and use fresh oil for the shrimp fry.

1. PREPARE THE WALNUTS: In a small pot over high heat, bring the water to a boil. Add the walnuts and blanch for 1 minute. Pour the walnuts into a colander set in the sink. Shake the colander while running cold water over the nuts. This will help remove the bitter skins.

2. In a small bowl, toss the walnuts with the sugar. The walnuts will have a bit of residual water, so the sugar should stick easily.

3. FRY THE WALNUTS: Pour oil to a depth of at least 2 inches (or halfway up the sides, whichever is shallower) into a small pot and heat over medium-high heat to 350°F. Line a baking sheet with parchment paper and set it near the stove.

4. Working in two to three batches, gently lower the walnuts into the oil and fry until they start to candy and turn dark brown, about 1 minute. Once they are removed from the pot, they will darken further as they cool, so don't let them fry too long. Using a slotted spoon, transfer to the prepared baking sheet to drain.

WALNUTS

4 cups water

1 cup walnut halves

¼ cup sugar

Neutral oil, preferably grapeseed, for frying (see Note)

2 teaspoons toasted sesame seeds

¼ teaspoon kosher salt

⅛ teaspoon MSG

5. Spread the hot walnuts in a single layer on the baking sheet. Sprinkle evenly with the sesame seeds, salt, and MSG. Set aside to cool for 30 minutes. As they cool, the walnuts will form a hard, sugary candied crust. (This step can be done a week in advance. Just store the nuts in an airtight container in the fridge until you're ready to make the rest of the dish.)

6. PREPARE THE SAUCE: In a large bowl, whisk together the mayonnaise, condensed milk, vinegar, and honey until well mixed. Set aside.

7. PREPARE THE BROCCOLI: Break the broccoli florets down to a size similar to the shrimp. Bring a small pot about half full of water to a boil over high heat. Add the broccoli and boil until the stems turn bright green, about 2 minutes. Using a slotted spoon, transfer the broccoli to a small bowl and season with salt and MSG to taste, tossing to coat.

8. FRY THE SHRIMP: Pour oil to a depth of at least 3 inches (or halfway up the sides, whichever is shallower) into a large pot or Dutch oven and heat to 350°F over medium-high heat.

9. While the oil heats, put the cornstarch into a wide, shallow dish. One or two at a time, thoroughly dust the shrimp with the cornstarch on both sides, shaking off the excess, and set aside on a plate.

10. Working in small batches to avoid crowding, gently lower the shrimp into the oil one at a time and fry, stirring occasionally to prevent the shrimp from sticking to one another or the bottom of the pot, until opaque and fully curled up, about 2 minutes. Using a slotted spoon, transfer the shrimp to the mayonnaise–condensed milk mixture and toss until well mixed. Repeat until all the shrimp are cooked.

11. TO SERVE THE SHRIMP: You can plate this dish however you like, but I like to make it look like it belongs in a Chinese banquet hall: layer the orange slices in a circle around the edge of a large plate, spoon the seasoned broccoli florets into the center of the orange circle, and pile the fried shrimp and candied walnuts on top of the broccoli. Garnish with toasted white sesame seeds and serve immediately.

SAUCE

1 cup Kewpie mayonnaise

2½ tablespoons sweetened condensed milk

2 tablespoons rice vinegar

1 tablespoon honey

BROCCOLI

1 medium head broccoli, cut into florets

Kosher salt

MSG

SHRIMP

Neutral oil, preferably grapeseed, for frying (see Note)

½ cup cornstarch

20 jumbo shrimp (U16/20), peeled and deveined

TO SERVE

2 oranges, unpeeled, thinly sliced into half-moons

Toasted white sesame seeds

LOBSTER CANTONESE

SERVES 2 TO 4

Have you ever ordered shrimp and lobster sauce and wondered where the lobster was? Your local restaurant wasn't trying to bait and switch you; it isn't running some sort of evil seafood scam. Many believe that in this Americanized Chinese dish, "lobster sauce" is simply paying homage to the glossy sauce of a traditional lobster Cantonese. The sauce is easy to make, but every ingredient plays a crucial role, from the ground pork that adds fatty richness and the deep flavor of the broth to the ribbons of egg that add a silky texture to the final sauce— perfect for clinging to hunks of chopped lobster. Lobster Cantonese is delicious, but the gravy-like pork sauce is the star in my opinion, which is impressive considering it's a whole lobster dish.

Note
Store the lobster in the coldest part of your fridge overnight or for up 2 days at most. You want it to be fresh, so it's best to buy it the day you plan to cook it. Live lobsters can be intimidating. But I'm here to hold your hand through this process. When it's time to break down the lobster, pop it into the freezer for 15 to 30 minutes (any longer and you risk degrading the quality of the meat) to lull it to sleep. Many consider this to be the most humane way to butcher a lobster. From there it's just a few simple chops with a cleaver or super-sharp, super-heavy knife. The shell of the lobster helps to flavor the sauce as it cooks, and it's easy to snag pieces off the plate with your chopsticks.

1. BREAK DOWN THE LOBSTER: Using your hands, separate the lobster tail from the body with one swift, clean twist. Using a cleaver or heavy chef's knife on a sturdy cutting board, split the tail lengthwise evenly in half. Chop each half crosswise into three equal pieces, then set aside. Using your hands, twist to remove the head and claws from the body. Using a pair of scissors, trim the gills from the body. Cut the body into four even pieces, halving in both directions, and then set the pieces aside. Using your hands, separate the knuckles from the claws with a quick twisting motion. (Use the back of the knife to smash the knuckle gently to make it easier to eat later.) Split the claws in half lengthwise down the center where the pincers come together. Discard the head (Or, if you like, use a spoon to scrape out the tomalley from the head into the pan at step 3, when adding the pork. Then add the head into the pot with the lobster pieces at step 4.) See step-by-step images on page 234.

1 (1½- to 2-pound) live lobster (see Note)

¼ pound ground pork (preferably 70/30 fat ratio)

1 tablespoon oyster sauce

½ teaspoon kosher salt

½ teaspoon MSG

¼ teaspoon sugar

⅛ teaspoon freshly ground white pepper

2 tablespoons neutral oil, preferably grapeseed

1 tablespoon minced ginger

5 garlic cloves, minced

2 scallions, thinly sliced

1 tablespoon Shaoxing wine

1 cup Cantonese Chicken Broth (page 29) or water

1 tablespoon water

1 tablespoon cornstarch

½ teaspoon toasted sesame oil

1 large egg, beaten

2 tablespoons unsalted butter

Fresh cilantro leaves, to garnish

2. In a small bowl, combine the pork, oyster sauce, salt, MSG, sugar, and pepper and mix well.

3. In a large pot, heat the neutral oil over medium-high heat. Once the oil is shimmering, add the pork mixture. Using a spatula, break up the pork into small chunks and cook, stirring every so often, until browned, about 4 minutes. When the pork is almost fully cooked, add the ginger, garlic, and scallions and cook, stirring occasionally, until the aromatics start to soften and take on a little color, about 3 minutes.

4. Add the lobster pieces to the pot and toss to coat in the gingery ground pork. Pour in the wine and deglaze the pot, using a spoon to scrape up all the delicious browned bits on the bottom of the pot and stir those flavorful pieces back into the sauce. Pour in the broth, cover the pot, and cook the lobster until the shells turn bright red, about 2 minutes.

5. In a small bowl, make a slurry by whisking together the water, cornstarch, and sesame oil until smooth. Remove the lid and drizzle in the slurry around the edge of the pot. Stir the slurry into the brothy sauce and simmer to thicken, about 1 minute.

6. Once the sauce has thickened, remove the pot from the heat and drizzle in the egg around the edge of the pot to cook gently and thicken the sauce further, about 2 minutes. The egg should create an almost ribbony texture in the sauce.

7. With the pot still off the heat, stir in the butter until fully melted and incorporated into the smooth and silky sauce. Garnish with cilantro and serve immediately.

SEAFOOD

SALT SUGAR MSG

SEAFOOD

8
SWEETS

I didn't grow up in a household with freshly baked chocolate chip cookies on the counter when I came home from school. Honestly, most Cantonese folks don't typically gravitate toward overly sweet desserts. More often than not, dinners at our house ended with a steamy mug of Ovaltine or a plate of fresh-cut fruit—a true show of a mother's love. But now I live with someone who has a sweet tooth to rival my salt tooth, in a household filled with treats. I still love my plate of fruit, but a person can grow. A person can change. Now I'm the type of person to end every meal with a hot fudge ice cream sundae (page 251) and slivers of steamed sponge cake (page 259) and spoonfuls of sweet, coconutty taro dessert soup (page 242) eaten straight from the container stashed in the back of the fridge.

A Guide to Fruit Plates	239
And a Bonus Recipe for MSG Caramel Dipper	240
Coconut Taro Sago Dessert Soup	242
Toasted Sesame Shortbread	244
No-Churn Yuen Yeung Ice Cream Cake	248
Salty, Malty Hot Fudge Sundae	251
Sweetened Egg Custard with Ginger Honey Syrup	252
Black Currant Lemonade Jelly Mold	256
Steamed Sponge Cake with Orange and Almond	259

A GUIDE TO FRUIT PLATES

A great gift, if you want to impress a Chinese mom, is a basketful of shiny, round oranges with the leafy green stems still intact.

The citrus is meant to resemble gold and is thought to bring happiness and good luck. That's why most Chinese banquets end with fresh-cut slices of orange served alongside the bill.

At Bonnie's, our fruit plate has been one of the two mainstays on the dessert menu since opening night. It's also one of the only dishes that's constantly changing, hinging on seasonality and what ripe fruit we picked up from Chinatown that week. Like snowflakes, no two fruit plates will ever look the same, but that's the fun of them. Our cooks are able to use their creativity and the plethora of ripe produce at hand to create something new every day. The fruit platter served to guests at 9:00 p.m. may not have the same fruit that adorned diners' plates at 5:00 p.m., but all the pieces were hand selected with the same love and care and attention, just the way a Chinese mom would make it. Health is wealth after all. And Chinese people take their health, wealth, and fruit very seriously.

This is more of a guide than a recipe. There aren't really any steps or instructions. You can truly mix and match whatever fruit you enjoy eating (I like to find a balance of varying textures and levels of sweetness and tartness). The most important thing is to spend time in the produce aisle selecting ripe, juicy fruit. There are different signs of ripeness for different fruits, so don't be afraid to pick up a pear to give it a squeeze or a sniff. You should use all your senses to determine when a piece of fruit is at its prime. Generally speaking . . .

HEAVY FRUIT IS JUICY FRUIT

Look for fruits that feel heavy for their size. Those will make for juicy bites.

SWEET FRUIT IS DOTTED WITH SMALL, LIGHT BROWN SPOTS

The spots are a sign the starches underneath the skin's surface are becoming sugary and sweet. On the other hand, bigger, darker bruised spots can be a sign of rot.

SOFT FRUIT IS READY-TO-EAT FRUIT

Look for fruit that has a little give but is not so soft that you're able to break or bruise the skin easily. Too soft and mushy could be overripe or rotten, whereas too firm usually means the fruit isn't ripe enough yet.

STRONG, SWEETLY PERFUMED FRUIT IS RIPE FRUIT

Oftentimes when ripe fruit is ready to eat, you can smell it immediately. Underripe fruit will not have much of a scent.

When it's time to build your fruit plate, always think about how your guests will eat each piece of fruit, with the main goal of making it easy for them. You want the fruit to still be recognizable (unless you have some incredible fruit-carving skills in your back pocket) while also being aesthetically pleasing. It is a centerpiece moment after all. Some fruits look beautiful with the skin still intact, like apples or pears thinly sliced and then fanned out. Other fruits, such as dragon fruit or mango, are best sliced away from the skin but still served in it for a fun pop-up of color. For rambutans or dragon eyes, I like to pull the peel back a bit to reveal the interior textures. A bunch of grapes makes for a wonderful filler in any awkward gaps on the plate. And I'm obsessed with soccer-mom orange slices tucked along the edges.

AND A BONUS RECIPE FOR
MSG Caramel Dipper

In a small pot over medium heat, combine 1 cup sugar, ½ cup water, 2 tablespoons light corn syrup, 1½ teaspoons kosher salt, and 1 teaspoon MSG. Slowly swirl the pot but don't stir as the sugar begins to caramelize and turn an amber golden brown, about 15 minutes. Meanwhile, in a microwave-safe bowl, gently warm ½ cup heavy cream in the microwave for 10 to 20 seconds to fully take the chill off. When the sugar mixture is ready, reduce the heat to low and slowly pour in the warmed cream. The caramel will bubble up. Immediately stir and scrape the sides and bottom of the pot using a rubber spatula. Once the bubbling subsides, remove the pot from the heat and stir in 2 tablespoons room-temperature unsalted butter until fully incorporated. The caramel should be smooth and silky and golden. You should have about 1½ cups. If you want, sprinkle it with a little Maldon flaky salt before serving immediately as a dipping sauce for apple slices and strawberries, or pour it over a bowl of vanilla ice cream. Store leftovers in an airtight container in the fridge for up to one week. To reheat for serving, warm in the microwave in 20-second bursts, stirring after each burst, for about 1 minute.

COCONUT TARO SAGO DESSERT SOUP

SERVES 4 TO 6

The final course of a Chinese banquet meal before the check is presented and the orange slices are devoured is often a dessert soup, usually either a lightly sweetened red bean soup or a coconut taro sago soup. It's the kitchen's choice, not the diner's. I always hope they send out the latter. I love the sweet nuttiness from the taro, the creaminess from the coconut, and the chew from the plump sago pearls. It's luscious and soupy served warm at the banquet hall but almost better eaten lukewarm, straight from the take-out container, when the soup has set into a more pudding-like texture.

Tip
Another fun way to serve this dessert is to ditch the steamed toppings and ladle the coconutty sago pudding over a warm, cracked-open roasted purple sweet potato.

1. In a medium pot, bring a steamer setup (see page 43) to a boil over high heat.

2. Meanwhile, cook the sago pearls according to the package instructions. Drain the pearls in a fine-mesh strainer and rinse under cold running water to remove any excess starchiness. Place the pearls in a small bowl filled with cold water and set aside.

3. Add the taro and sweet potato to a 7- to 9-inch steaming tray. Carefully lower the steaming tray onto the steaming rack. Cover and steam the pieces until they are slightly tender but still have a little bite to them, 10 to 12 minutes. Remove the tray from the steamer setup and set aside.

4. In a medium pot over medium-high heat, combine the evaporated milk, coconut milk, condensed milk, sugar, and salt and bring to a boil, whisking every couple of minutes to prevent the dairy from scorching on the bottom of the pot. When the mixture is at a boil, drain the sago pearls and add them to the pot, then give the mixture a good stir to disperse the sago evenly throughout the soup. Remove from the heat.

5. The soup will thicken as it cools because of the starches in the sago pearls, so for a looser soup texture, serve the soup warm in big bowls topped with the chunks of steamed taro and sweet potato. For a thicker, more pudding-like texture, let the soup cool down before adding the toppings.

½ cup sago or small tapioca pearls (not quick cooking)

½ pound taro, peeled and cut into small dice

1 small purple sweet potato, peeled and cut into small dice

2 cups evaporated milk

1 cup unsweetened coconut milk (I like Chaokoh brand)

¼ cup sweetened condensed milk

¼ cup sugar

¼ teaspoon kosher salt

TOASTED SESAME SHORTBREAD

MAKES 36 COOKIES

I have a soft spot for sesame-flavored Chinese treats: nutty *jian dui*, fried sesame balls filled with sticky, jammy lotus seed paste or red bean paste; chewy steamed black sesame rolls plucked from the rolling carts at dim sum halls; brittle sesame peanut candy that almost glues your mouth shut and yanks your cavities out in an oddly satisfying way. But most of the time when I crave that sesame flavor, I don't really feel like frying or steaming or making candy. So here's my shortcut, a buttery, not-too-sweet, sesame-forward shortbread cookie. Tender and delicate, these cookies are rolled in a sugary, toasty black-and-white sesame seed mix to create a crunchy, sparkly crust—not traditional but still satisfying that sesame craving.

Tip
These shortbread logs can be made ahead and stored, tightly wrapped in plastic wrap, for up to 1 week in the fridge or up to 1 month in the freezer. You can bake off the cookies and then store them in an airtight container for up to 5 days.

1 cup (2 sticks/227g) unsalted butter, cubed, at room temperature

½ cup (100g) granulated sugar

¼ cup (53g) packed dark brown sugar

½ teaspoon (1.5g) kosher salt

1 large egg, separated

1 tablespoon (14g) toasted sesame oil

2¼ cups (270g) all-purpose flour

2 tablespoons demerara sugar, for rolling

2 tablespoons toasted white sesame seeds, for rolling

2 tablespoons toasted black sesame seeds, for rolling

1. In a stand mixer fitted with the paddle attachment (or in a large bowl with a handheld electric mixer), beat together the butter, granulated sugar, brown sugar, and salt on medium-high speed until all the streaks of butter disappear into the mixture, about 3 minutes.

2. Use a rubber spatula to scrape down the sides of the bowl, then add the egg yolk and oil and beat on low speed just until blended. Add the flour and continue to beat on low speed until fully incorporated, 30 to 45 seconds. Scrape down the bowl sides one more time to ensure the flour is fully incorporated.

3. Lay two long pieces of plastic wrap on a work surface. Divide the dough into roughly even halves and dump one onto each piece of plastic wrap. Using your hands, shape each piece of dough into a rough log about 6 inches long and 2 inches in diameter. Wrap up each log in the plastic wrap and then give each wrapped log a few good squeezes and rolls to make sure it's holding together and has a nice evenly rounded shape. Place the dough in the fridge until it's firm enough to slice, about 1½ hours (see Tip).

4. When ready to bake the cookies, position two racks in the center of the oven and preheat the oven to 350°F. Line 2 baking sheets with parchment paper.

5. In a small bowl, stir together the demerara sugar and white and black sesame seeds. Sprinkle the mixture on a piece of parchment paper large enough to fit the dough logs or on another baking sheet. In another small bowl, beat the egg white until homogenous. Pull the dough from the fridge and unwrap a log. Brush the log on all sides with the egg white, then roll it in the sugary sesame mixture, coating the sides completely. If there are any bare spots, use your hands to pack on the sugar mixture to cover them. Repeat with the second dough log.

6. Cut the dough logs crosswise into ⅓-inch-thick slices and lay the slices on the prepared baking sheets, spacing them about ½ inch apart. You should have about 36 cookies.

7. Bake the cookies, switching the pans between the racks and rotating the pans back to front halfway through, until the bottoms turn lightly golden brown, 15 to 17 minutes. Let cool on the pans on wire racks for a few minutes before eating.

NO-CHURN YUEN YEUNG ICE CREAM CAKE

SERVES 8 TO 10

If it's your birthday in the Eng household, there will always be a cake, but it will never be homemade. My family loves a Carvel ice cream cake covered in sugary frosting and layered with chocolate crunchies sliced into big, melty chunks, the leftovers quickly tucked away into old plastic take-out containers to keep in the freezer. That's why it almost feels silly to write a recipe for an ice cream cake when Carvel is just so consistently good. But this is a cheater's version, made with layers of a classic Asian household staple, frozen Sara Lee pound cake, and a simple no-churn ice cream flavored with black tea and instant coffee, riffing on a steaming mug of *yuen yeung* (page 74). We'll probably still wind up getting a Carvel cake every time someone's special day rolls around, but we could always start a new tradition with two birthday cakes on the table too.

1. MAKE THE YUEN YEUNG NO-CHURN ICE CREAM BASE:
In a small pot over medium heat, combine 1 cup of the cream and the tea and bring to a simmer. Reduce the heat to low so the cream is just barely steaming and steep the tea in the cream uncovered for 20 minutes.

2. Pass the steeped cream through a fine-mesh strainer over a medium bowl, using the back of a spoon to press every bit of infused cream through the strainer. Discard the spent tea leaves. Cover the bowl and place the steeped cream in the fridge to chill and thicken up for at least 1 hour or up to 3 hours.

3. Remove the chilled steeped cream from the refrigerator and add the remaining 1 cup cream and the coffee powder to the bowl. Whisk the cream mixture by hand or with an electric mixer on medium speed just until barely stiff peaks form, 5 to 6 minutes (potentially longer if you are whisking by hand).

4. In a small bowl, stir together the condensed milk, coconut oil, and salt, mixing well.

YUEN YEUNG NO-CHURN ICE CREAM

2 cups heavy cream, divided

¼ cup Lipton orange pekoe loose leaf tea

1 tablespoon instant coffee powder

⅔ cup sweetened condensed milk

2 tablespoons refined coconut oil

¼ teaspoon kosher salt

5. Take a big spoonful of the whipped cream and add it to the condensed milk mixture. Using a rubber spatula, give a few good stirs to lighten the condensed milk mixture. It should be noticeably easier to stir. Gently fold all the lightened condensed milk mixture into the whipped cream, taking care not to knock too much air out of the whipped cream.

6. PREPARE THE ICE CREAM CAKE: Remove the pound cake from the aluminum tin. Line the tin with plastic wrap, leaving a 2-inch overhang on the long sides. Using a serrated knife, slice the pound cake horizontally into three (evenish) layers. Place the bottom slice of the pound cake into the lined loaf tin.

7. Spoon half of the no-churn ice cream over the bottom layer of the pound cake. Add the middle layer of the pound cake, followed by the remainder of the no-churn ice cream. Top with the final layer of cake and gently press down on the top. Cover the top of the cake with the plastic wrap overhang, then place the assembled cake in the freezer until firm, at least 4 hours or up to 2 weeks.

8. JUST BEFORE SERVING, PREPARE THE WHIPPED CREAM: In a medium bowl, combine the cream and sugar (if using) and whisk together by hand or with an electric mixer on medium speed until supersoft peaks form, 4 to 5 minutes (potentially longer if you are whisking by hand).

9. Remove the cake from the freezer about 10 minutes before you plan to serve. Fold back the plastic wrap from the top, then use the overhang to lift the cake from the tin. Cut into eight to ten slices and serve immediately with dollops of the whipped cream.

CAKE

1 (16-ounce) Sara Lee Classic Pound Cake

½ cup heavy cream

1 tablespoon sugar (optional)

SALTY, MALTY HOT FUDGE SUNDAE

SERVES 6 TO 8

In the months leading up to the grand opening of Bonnie's, I had ice cream every single night. Phoebe and I had just moved in together, and it seemed only wise that I, a loving, doting boyfriend, join in on her nighttime routine. Sometimes it was a single scoop in a bowl; other nights it was a spoon straight into the pint. Occasionally, there were chocolate sprinkles, a few chunks of fresh strawberries, or slices of banana. Every once in a while, she topped the scoop with a warm and gooey chocolate chip cookie, melting the ice cream away into a puddle. Those nights inspired me to put a fully loaded sundae on the dessert menu when the restaurant finally opened: a bowl of vanilla ice cream topped with fried milk cubes and smothered in spoonfuls of hot fudge spiked with malty, chocolaty Ovaltine, a *cha chaan teng* classic and the same malted powder I grew up stirring into warmed milk for my nighttime sweet treat years before Phoebe and I met.

Tip
Store the hot fudge in an airtight container in the fridge for up to a week if you don't plan to use it right away. Reheat in a microwave in 10-second bursts, stirring after each burst, until loose, warm, and ready for ice cream.

1. MAKE THE HOT FUDGE: In a small pot over medium heat, whisk together the cream, Ovaltine powder, sugar, corn syrup, malt powder, and water until everything is dissolved and the mixture is silky smooth.

2. Insert a candy thermometer into the liquid, bring the mixture to a boil, and cook until the thermometer registers 220°F, about 6 minutes. Remove the pot from the heat, add the chocolate, and stir until the chocolate melts and the sauce is smooth. Whisk in the butter, vanilla, and salt until the sauce emulsifies. Strain through a fine-mesh strainer to ensure the hot fudge is supersmooth. Keep warm (or see Tip).

3. TO ASSEMBLE EACH SUNDAE: In a big ice cream bowl, layer two or three scoops of the ice cream flavor(s) of your choosing, followed by a big spoonful of hot fudge, a layer of chopped nuts, whipped cream, sprinkles, pork floss, a final layer of chopped nuts, and a cherry, according to your preference. Serve immediately.

SALTY, MALTY OVALTINE HOT FUDGE

¾ cup heavy cream

7 tablespoons Ovaltine Malted Drink powder (I like European Formula)

5 tablespoons packed dark brown sugar

5 tablespoons light corn syrup

2 tablespoons malt powder

2 tablespoons water

½ cup coarsely chopped dark chocolate (65 to 75 percent cacao)

1½ tablespoons unsalted butter

1 teaspoon pure vanilla extract

1 teaspoon kosher salt

SUNDAE

2 to 3 pints of vanilla, chocolate, or strawberry ice cream

¼ cup chopped unsalted roasted nuts of your choice (optional)

Whipped cream

Rainbow sprinkles (optional)

Pork floss (optional)

Maraschino cherries

SWEETS

SWEETENED EGG CUSTARD
with Ginger Honey Syrup

SERVES 2 TO 4

The tofu shop around the corner from my grandparents' apartment scooped fresh, warm tofu pudding into deli containers sold with small cups of ginger honey syrup to pour over top. The syrup was sweet and hot in that way ginger can be, the ideal balance of spice. The bakery on the other side of the block served warm-from-the-oven egg tarts. Their jiggly, custardy, barely set center felt like it could practically spill out from the shell after the first bite. So this dessert is a true mash-up of the best parts of my favorite Chinatown sweets: a wobbly sweetened egg custard served warm straight from the steamer topped with big spoonfuls of ginger honey syrup spiked with star anise and a cinnamon stick.

Tip
Save any leftover ginger honey syrup to spoon over a scoop of vanilla ice cream.

1. PREPARE THE SWEETENED EGG CUSTARD: In a small pot over medium-high heat, combine the water and granulated sugar. Swirl the pot to dissolve the sugar, then bring the mixture to a boil, boil for 30 seconds, and remove from the heat. Set this simple syrup aside to cool down for 10 minutes.

2. In a large pot, bring a steamer setup (see page 43) to a rapid simmer over medium-high heat.

3. In a medium bowl, whisk together the eggs, egg yolk, evaporated milk, and vanilla until blended. Pour in the cooled simple syrup and whisk until the mixture is silky smooth. Set a fine-mesh strainer over a 7- to 9-inch steaming tray and pass the egg mixture through the strainer to remove any stray egg white clumps or bits of shell. Use a spoon to gently skim and discard any bubbles on top.

4. Lay a long sheet of plastic wrap on the counter, then gently place the custard-filled steaming tray on one end of the plastic wrap. Bring the remaining plastic wrap over the top of the tray to meet the bottom in one continuous tight sheet. Wrap as tightly as possible to prevent moisture from getting in.

SWEETENED EGG CUSTARD

1 cup water

3 tablespoons granulated sugar

2 large eggs, plus 1 large egg yolk

½ cup evaporated milk

½ teaspoon pure vanilla extract

5. Carefully lower the steaming tray onto the steaming rack. Cover and steam the egg custard for 15 minutes. Be patient and wait the full 15 minutes before lifting the lid to check on the custard. You're looking for the top of the custard to be smooth and uniform, with a tiny jiggle under the surface. Remove the tray from the steamer setup and allow it to rest for 1 minute before removing the plastic wrap.

6. WHILE THE CUSTARD STEAMS, PREPARE THE GINGER HONEY SYRUP: In a small pot over medium heat, combine the water, honey, ginger, brown sugar, star anise, and cinnamon stick and bring to a simmer. Simmer the mixture, swirling the pan occasionally, until it reduces to a maple syrup–like viscosity, 6 to 7 minutes. Remove from the heat and discard the ginger, star anise, and cinnamon stick.

7. TO SERVE: Spoon as much of the ginger honey syrup over the top of the warm egg custard as you like. Sprinkle with a pinch of flaky salt and dig in.

GINGER HONEY SYRUP

¼ cup water

¼ cup honey

1 (1-inch) piece ginger, smashed

1 tablespoon packed dark brown sugar

1 star anise

1 cinnamon stick

Maldon flaky salt, to serve

BLACK CURRANT LEMONADE JELLY MOLD

SERVES 8

Chinese people love jellied textures in their food. The gelatinous silky skin of a cold poached chicken (page 206), the chewy bite of a braised tendon, the slippery jiggle of an almond or grass jelly. So when I was thinking about recipes for this dessert chapter, I knew I wanted to include some sort of jellied dessert. A cubed jelly, a jellied pudding, a mold—the form didn't really matter as long as the flavor was banging. Enter sweet and syrupy Ribena black currant juice, a punchy concentrate that made its way from Britain to the drink menu of nearly every *cha chaan teng* in Hong Kong. It's super tasty diluted into sparkling water and served with a wheel of lemon or, my personal favorite, stirred into sour lemonade. And after months of testing flavors for this molded dessert, I learned that this sweet-tart combo is equally (if not more) tasty when layered. The Ribena layer gets the classic Jell-O treatment, while the lemonade layer has a touch of sweetened condensed milk stirred into it right before setting and chilling to create a more luxurious mouthfeel. The result is delicious and fun to look at—what more could you want from a Jell-O dessert?

Tip
If the mold was properly greased, the jelly should easily slide from it. But if you are having any trouble, you can dip the exterior of the mold into a bowl of warm water for 10-second dunks until the sides loosen a touch and the jelly will slide from the mold.

½ teaspoon neutral oil, preferably grapeseed

2 cups Ribena black currant juice, divided

1 tablespoon plus 1½ teaspoons gelatin powder, divided

¾ cup freshly squeezed lemon juice

⅓ cup water

¾ cup sweetened condensed milk

1. Using a paper towel, thoroughly grease a 4-cup Jell-O mold with the oil. (I love the look of a fish mold, but you can use any 4-cup Jell-O mold, Bundt pan, or baking dish.) If you are using a fish mold (or another mold that won't sit upright on its own), build a small nest of aluminum foil in a slightly bigger dish to hold it steady so the layers set even and flat.

2. PREPARE THE BLACK CURRANT LAYER: In a small pot over medium heat, whisk together 1 cup of the black currant juice and 1 tablespoon of the gelatin until the gelatin dissolves, whisking continuously until all the lumps are gone. Remove the pot from the heat and stir in the remaining 1 cup black currant juice to cool down the mixture.

3. Pour the black currant jelly into the prepared mold, then pop the mold into the fridge to set the jelly until the center is fairly firm to the touch but still jiggly, about 2 hours.

4. PREPARE THE LEMONADE LAYER: In a small pot over medium heat, whisk together the lemon juice, water, and the remaining 1½ teaspoons gelatin until the gelatin dissolves, whisking continuously until all the lumps are gone. Remove the pot from the heat and set aside to cool down completely.

5. When the black currant layer is set, whisk the condensed milk into the lemonade mixture. Do not add the condensed milk to the lemonade mixture while it is still hot or it will curdle, leaving little white lumps in the jelly mold. Carefully spoon the lemonade mixture over the black currant layer, creating an even coating.

6. Pop the mold back into the fridge to set up until firm, another 3 to 4 hours. When it's ready, unmold (see Tip) and serve.

STEAMED SPONGE CAKE
with Orange and Almond

SERVES 8 TO 10

Steaming a cake may sound intimidating if you're more accustomed to the oven route, but as you've learned in this book, you can steam pretty much anything and everything. The passive, moist heat makes for a lovely cake with a spongy, featherlight texture. As a kid I loved nothing more than to break out my mom's old-school pink Sunbeam Mixmaster and whip eggs into sugar and a bit of flour to create the frothy cake batter. In fact, when I was ten years old, I made a version of this cake so often that my grandma at one point had to firmly request that I stop making it for her.

I've tweaked the list of ingredients a tad from that original recipe, updating the flavor profile from a more traditional vanilla with a smattering of sesame seeds to a few teaspoons of orange zest rubbed into the sugar, a dash of almond extract, and a light dusting of powdered sugar, transforming what was once a lovely afternoon steamed snacking cake served with a pot of tea to a full-on dessert moment. I wish I could make this for my grandma. Who knows, maybe she'd actually request I make it again.

1. Grate the zest of the orange into a small bowl. Add the granulated sugar and, using your fingers, rub the zest into the sugar to coat the sugar with the citrusy oils. Set aside the orange.

2. PREPARE THE CAKE BATTER: In a stand mixer fitted with the whisk attachment, beat the eggs on high speed until foamy, about 2 minutes. With the machine running, add the orange sugar and beat until the mixture is light and frothy and almost tripled in volume, about 2 minutes.

3. Wand almond and vanilla extracts and then beat until everything is fully incorporated and frothy, about 1 minute. Turn off the mixer.

4. In a small bowl, whisk together the cake flour, baking powder, and baking soda. Sift the flour mixture into the egg mixture and then add the salt. Turn on the mixer to low speed and gently mix the batter until it is smooth with no lumps or flour streaks, about 45 seconds. Give the batter a few good stirs by hand using a rubber spatula to make sure everything is well mixed before covering the bowl with plastic wrap and letting the batter rest at room temperature for 30 minutes. You should notice lots of airy bubbles rising to the surface. This is a good sign that the baking soda and baking powder are activating.

1 large orange

¾ cup (150g) granulated sugar

4 large eggs, at room temperature

½ cup (130g) evaporated milk

⅓ cup (75g) neutral oil, preferably grapeseed, plus more for greasing

2 teaspoons (8g) pure almond extract

2 teaspoons (8g) pure vanilla extract

1 cup plus 2 tablespoons (135g) cake flour

2 teaspoons (8g) baking powder

½ teaspoon (3g) baking soda

⅛ teaspoon kosher salt

Powdered sugar, to dust

RECIPE CONTINUES

5. In a large pot, bring a steamer setup (see page 43) to a boil over high heat, then reduce the temperature to medium-high to bring the water to a rapid simmer. Lightly brush the bottom and sides of an 8-inch round nonstick cake pan with oil, then line the bottom with a round of parchment paper. Right before steaming, remove the pot lid and wrap a thick kitchen towel around the lid, knotting the corners under the handle, to create a tight seal. This will prevent any condensation from dripping onto the cake as it steams.

6. STEAM THE CAKE: Gently scrape the batter into the prepared cake pan and carefully lower the pan onto the steaming rack. Cover and steam the cake until it's gently domed and springy to the touch, 38 to 40 minutes. Remove the pan from the steamer setup and let cool for 10 to 15 minutes. Then run a thin knife blade around the inside edge of the pan to release the cake from the pan's side. Turn the cake out onto a wire rack, peel off the parchment, and then turn upright. Let cool completely.

7. TO SERVE: Peel the reserved orange by hand, then thinly slice into ⅛-inch-thick rounds. Arrange the orange slices on top of the cake. Lightly dust the top with powdered sugar just before serving.

ACKNOWLEDGMENTS

Straight up, this book would not have become a reality if it wasn't for my fiancé, Phoebe. (Maybe by the time you're reading this, you'll finally be my wife, but at this very moment we haven't been able to find a free second in our busy lives to get to city hall to make it official.) Phoebe, you are the most dedicated, smart, creative, organized badass who understands me probably better than I understand myself. I don't know why anyone would willingly sign up to write a cookbook while 8 months pregnant and then stay up until the wee hours of the morning writing it all while working a full-time job and figuring out how to raise a little human being. But you did. I'm not sure how I could ever really thank you for getting sucked into this journey with me and giving it your all, but I owe you everything. So thank you, Phoebe.

Thank you, Mommy, you taught me everything I know about Cantonese food. Without you, there would be no "Cantonese" in my cooking. You are my Google, my Reddit, my encyclopedia of all things Cantonese food. Thank you for always translating condiment jar labels I can't read, telling me where to buy the best *ham yue*, and pointing out which aunties sell the best produce.

Thank you to the whole Clarkson Potter team, who helped turn these words into a book. Thank you to our editor, Jenn Sit. You offered such incredible and thoughtful guidance throughout this entire cookbook writing process. Phoebe and I truly had no idea what I was signing us up for when I decided I wanted to write a cookbook, but you held our hands throughout every stage. It was an honor to work with a fellow Cantonese American who understood my vision, my food, and my story. Thank you to Emily Stephenson for such kind, detailed recipe notes, and thank you to Robert Diaz for taking our muddled mood board and turning it into something so beautiful.

Thank you to our photographer, Alex Lau, for shooting this book. I have been a fan of your work for so many years and feel so fortunate to not only have worked with you on this project but to also be able to call you my friend now. Thank you for telling me you actually thought my food tasted good. Thank you to our food stylist, Tyna Hoang, who led us through 6½ insanely busy, jam-packed days with such a wonderfully happy spirit. Thank you for making it all look so easy, even when I was hovering over your shoulder every second of the day. Thank you to our food stylist's assistant, Alyssa Kondracki, for spending days organizing, prepping, and cooking all the recipes in this book. But especially thank you for that crust on the Sweet Potato Curry Potpie. Thank you to our prop stylist, Nicole Louie, for rummaging through my mom's kitchen cabinets to steal props so this book would feel like home. Thank you for being so down to prop this book out with your own Rolex and twenty-five-year-old Styrofoam cups that my dad bought on sale back in 1999. Thank you all for holding our son when our arms got too tired, for making some of the ugliest looking dishes beautiful, and for just being so fun and kind and generous on set. There truly are not enough ways to say how much we appreciate you all (and how apologetic we are for shooting nineteen recipes that second to last day), but maybe we can take you all out to Roll and Roaster again one day soon?

Thank you to our talented recipe tester, Vivian Chan-Tam, for testing every single recipe in this book. We still can't believe you found the time to cook all these recipes when you had your second beautiful baby girl during our insane development phase. Thank you for calling when things didn't work or tasted too salty, thank you for leaving endless notes and tips, and thank you for pulling me out of my midsummer creative rut.

Thank you to our agent, Katherine Cowles. We couldn't believe you wanted to work with us when your talent list was made up of everyone we admire and respect in the cookbook world. Thank you for guiding us in the early phase of this project and for answering our phone calls at 11:00 p.m. on Saturday nights when we decided we hated everything we had written in our proposal.

Thank you to the entire crew at Bonnie's. There is truly no way I could have found the time to write this book if I didn't have such a trustworthy team to hold down the fort.

Thank you to our son, Levi. Thank you for being our most honest recipe tester, our most loyal fan, and our most important reason to take a break from working and go outside to play in the sun.

And if you got this far, thank you.
Thank you for giving this book a shot.

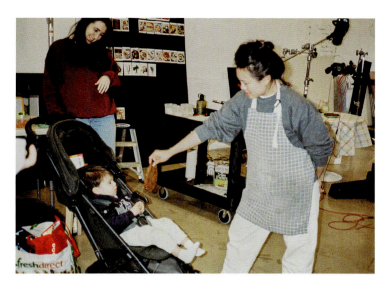

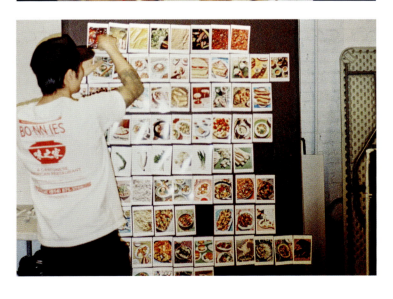

ACKNOWLEDGMENTS

INDEX

Note:
Page references in *italics* indicate photographs.

A

Almond and Orange, Steamed Sponge Cake with, *258*, 259–60
Anchovies, dried
   about, 17
   Fish Mix, *80*, 81
   XO Sauce, *33*, 37
Arancini, Congee, 146–47, *148*

B

Bacon
   BLT Fried Rice, 140, *141*
   Cantonese Minestrone, 128–29, *129*
   Clay Pot Rice (Without a Clay Pot), *149*, 150–51
   cured Chinese (lap yuk), 17
   Nam Yu Maple Candied, *54*, 55
   XO Sauce, *33*, 37
Bean curd, fermented. *See* Fuyu
Beans
   Cantonese Minestrone, 128–29, *129*
   Chinatown Crudités with Sour Cream and Green Onion Dip, 106, *107*
   dao gok, *104*
   Dao Gok with Fermented Bean Curd Garlic Butter, *116*, 117
Beef
   Brisket Noodle Soup, 182–83, *183*
   Burger, Black Pepper, *191*, 192–93
   Chow Fun, *178*, 179–80
   Crispy Sheet Pan Fried Noodles, *165*, 166–67
   Mini Sweet-and-Sour Meat Loaves, *202*, 203
   Steamed Silken Tofu with Beefy Black Bean Garlic Sauce, *200*, 201
Black Bean Garlic Sauce, *26*, 28
   Beefy, Steamed Silken Tofu with, *200*, 201
   Clams with, *226*, 227
Black Currant Lemonade Jelly Mold, *255*, 256–57
Black Pepper
   Beef Burger, *191*, 192–93
   Salt and Pepper Seasoning, *32*, 34
Black Sesame Milk, Iced, *72*, 73
Black soybeans, fermented
   about, 18
   Black Bean Garlic Sauce, *26*, 28
Bread
   Milk, Buns with Butter, 60–61, *61*
   Scallion Milk, Blankets, Piggies in, 96–97, *97*
   Stuffed Golden Lava French Toast with Salted Duck Egg Custard, 66–68, *67*
Broccoli, Chinese, *104*
   Clay Pot Rice (Without a Clay Pot), *149*, 150–51
Broth, Cantonese Chicken, *26*, 29
Buns, Milk Bread, with Butter, 60–61, *61*
Burger, Black Pepper Beef, *191*, 192–93

C

Cabbage
   Charred, with Shrimp Paste Butter, 114, *115*
   Ham Yue Yook Beng Stuffed, 189, *190*
   Salad with Fried Garlic Sesame Dressing, *108*, 109
Cakes
   No-Churn Yuen Yeung Ice Cream, *247*, 248–49
   Steamed Sponge, with Orange and Almond, *258*, 259–60
Candy/deep-fry thermometer, 39
Caramel Dipper, MSG, 240
Carbon-steel skillets, 39
Cast-iron skillets, 39
Cauliflower, Chinese, *105*
   Chinatown Crudités with Sour Cream and Green Onion Dip, 106, *107*
Celery, Chinese, *104*
   Cantonese Minestrone, 128–29, *129*
   Chinatown Crudités with Sour Cream and Green Onion Dip, 106, *107*
Cereal
   Fish Mix, *80*, 81
Charcuterie, Cantonese, 17
Cha Siu, Pomegranate Molasses, 212–14, *213*
Cheese
   Congee Arancini, 146–47, *148*
   Fuyu Cacio e Pepe Mein, 162–63, *164*
   and Ham Lo Bak Go, Crispy, 118–19, *119*
   Steamed Then Fried Egg Sandwich, *63*, 64–65
   Tinned Dace Dip, *84*, 85
Cheung Fun, XO, 176, *177*
Chicken
   Broth, Cantonese, *26*, 29
   Crispy Sheet Pan Fried Noodles, *165*, 166–67
   Poached, QQ's, 206–7, *208*
   poaching liquid, storing, 207
   Roast Duck (Without a Duck), *209*, 210–11
   Rotisserie, Congee, 144, *145*

267

Chicken (*continued*)
Sweet Potato Curry Potpie, 194–95, *196*
Thighs, Crispy, with Chips and Lemon, *197*, 198-99, *199*
Wings, Lemon Cola, 86, *87*
Chili
Green, Ginger Scallion Sauce, *27*, 31
Oil, Shrimp, *33*, 36
Chinese bacon. *See* Lap yuk
Chinese broccoli, *104*
Clay Pot Rice (Without a Clay Pot), *149*, 150–51
Crispy Sheet Pan Fried Noodles, *165*, 166–67
Chinese cauliflower, *105*
Chinatown Crudités with Sour Cream and Green Onion Dip, 106, *107*
Chinese celery, *104*
Cantonese Minestrone, 128–29, *129*
Chinatown Crudités with Sour Cream and Green Onion Dip, 106, *107*
Chinese sausage. *See* Lap cheong
Chives. *See* Garlic chives
Chocolate
Salty, Malty Ovaltine Hot Fudge, *250*, 251
Waffles, Malted, 58, *59*
Chowder, Corn, 126, *127*
Chow Fun, Beef, *178*, 179–80
Clams
with Black Bean Garlic Sauce, *226*, 227
Casino, 224–25, *225*
XO Seafood Lo Mai Fan, 154–55, *155*
Cleaver, 40
Coconut Taro Sago Dessert Soup, 242, *243*
Coffee Milk Tea, 74, *75*
Cola Lemon Chicken Wings, 86,*87*
Condiments, store-bought, 17–25
Congee
Arancini, 146–47, *148*
Ginger, *142*, 143
Rotisserie Chicken, 144, *145*
Cooking tips, 44–47
Corn
Canned, and Scallion Fried Rice, *138*, 139
Chowder, 126, *127*
Crackers
Fish Mix, *80*, 81
Cruller, Fried (Yauh Ja Gwai), 98–100, *99*
Custard
Salted Duck Egg, Stuffed Golden Lava French Toast with, 66–68, *67*

Steamed Egg, with Vinegary, Marinated Tomatoes, 122–24, *125*
Sweetened Egg, with Ginger Honey Syrup, 252–53, *254*
Cutting boards, 40

D

Daikon, *105*. *See also* Salted radish
Beef Brisket Noodle Soup, 182–83, *183*
Cantonese Minestrone, 128–29, *129*
Crispy Ham and Cheese Lo Bak Go, 118–19, *119*
Dao Gok, *104*
Chinatown Crudités with Sour Cream and Green Onion Dip, 106, *107*
with Fermented Bean Curd Garlic Butter, *116*, 117
Digital scale, 40
Dips
MSG Caramel Dipper, 240
Sour Cream and Green Onion, 106, *107*
Tinned Dace, *84*, 85
Dried anchovies
about, 17
Fish Mix, *80*, 81
XO Sauce, *33*, 37
Dried scallops
about, 17
Corn Chowder, 126, *127*
XO Seafood Lo Mai Fan, 154–55, *155*
Dried seafood, types of, 17
Dried shiitake mushrooms, about, 17
Dried shrimp
about, 17
Fish Mix, *80*, 81
Shrimp Chili Oil, *33*, 36
XO Sauce, *33*, 37
XO Seafood Lo Mai Fan, 154–55, *155*
Drinks
Coffee Milk Tea, 74, *75*
Iced Black Sesame Milk, *72*, 73
Milk Tea, 74
Soy Milk, 70, *71*
Duck, Roast (Without a Duck), *209*, 210–11
Duck Egg, Salted, Custard, Stuffed Golden Lava French Toast with, 66–68, *67*
Dumplings, Pork and Chive, with Caramelized Onion Soy Butter, *92–93*, 94–95

E

Egg(s)
BLT Fried Rice, 140, *141*
Canned Corn and Scallion Fried Rice, *138*, 139
Clay Pot Rice (Without a Clay Pot), *149*, 150–51
Custard, Steamed, with Vinegary, Marinated Tomatoes, 122–24, *125*
Custard, Sweetened, with Ginger Honey Syrup, 252–53, *254*
Ginger Congee, *142*, 143
Jammy Marble Tea, 82, *83*
Mac Soup Mac Salad, *160*, 161
Salted Duck, Custard, Stuffed Golden Lava
French Toast with, 66–68, *67*
Scramble, Hong Kong, 52, 53
Steamed Then Fried, Sandwich, *63*, 64–65
Wok-Fried, 50, *51*
Equipment list, 39–40
Evaporated milk, about, 18

F

Fermented bean curd. *See* Fuyu
Fermented black soybeans
about, 18
Black Bean Garlic Sauce, *26*, 28
Shrimp Chili Oil, *33*, 36
Fine-mesh strainer, 40
Fish. *See also* Anchovies
Fried, Lettuce, Tomato (FFLT) Sandwich, *220*, 221
Grilled Squid with Preserved Lemon, 222, *223*
Sizzling Steamed, with Seasoned Soy Sauce, 218, *219*
tinned dace, about, 25
Tinned Dace Dip, *84*, 85
Fish, salted preserved. *See* Ham Yue
Fish Mix, *80*, 81
French Toast, Stuffed Golden Lava, with Salted Duck Egg Custard, 66–68, *67*
Fruit. *See also specific fruits*
plates, a guide to, 239–40
Fuyu
about, 18

Cacio e Pepe Mein, 162–63, *164*
Dao Gok with Fermented Bean
 Curd Garlic Butter, *116*, 117

G

Garlic
 Black Bean Sauce, *26*, 28
 in Cantonese cooking, 14
 Fermented Bean Curd Butter, Dao
  Gok with, *116*, 117
 fried, about, 18
 Fried, Sesame Dressing, Cabbage
  Salad with, *108*, 109
 Prawns, Steamed, over Mung Bean
  Vermicelli, *168*, 169
 Salt and Pepper Seasoning, *32*, 34
Garlic chives, *105*
Ginger
 in Cantonese cooking, 14
 Congee, *142*, 143
 Green Chili Scallion Sauce, *27*, 31
 Honey Syrup, Sweetened Egg Cus-
  tard with, 252–53, *254*
 Sizzling Steamed Fish with Sea-
  soned Soy Sauce, 218, *219*
Green onions. *See* Scallion(s)

H

Ham
 and Cheese Lo Bak Go, Crispy,
  118–19, *119*
 Congee Arancini, 146–47, *148*
Ham Yue
 about, 21
 Yook Beng (Steamed Pork Patty
  with Salted Fish), 188–89, *189*
 Yook Beng Stuffed Cabbage, 189,
  190
Hash Browns, Taro Root Diner, with
 Sweet-and-Spicy Ketchup, *56*, 57
Hoisin sauce, about, 21
Honey Ginger Syrup, Sweetened Egg
 Custard with, 252–53, *254*
Hot dogs
 Piggies in Scallion Milk Bread
  Blankets, 96–97, *97*
Hot mustard powder
 about, 21

Chinese Hot Mustard, *27*, 30
Hup To Ha (Shrimp and Walnuts),
 228–29, *230*

I

Ice Cream
 Cake, No-Churn Yuen Yeung, *247*,
  248–49
 Salty, Malty Hot Fudge Sundae, *250*,
  251
Ingredients
 aromatics, 14
 salt, sugar, and MSG, 15
 store-bought sauces and condiments,
  17–25

J

Jelly Mold, Black Currant Lemonade,
 255, 256–57

K

Kewpie mayonnaise, about, 21

L

Lap cheong (Chinese sausage links)
 about, 17
 Clams Casino, 224–25, *225*
 Clay Pot Rice (Without a Clay Pot),
  149, 150–51
 XO Seafood Lo Mai Fan, 154–55, *155*
Lap yuk (Chinese bacon)
 about, 17
 Cantonese Minestrone, 128–29,
  129
 Clay Pot Rice (Without a Clay Pot),
  149, 150–51
Lemon
 Black Currant Lemonade Jelly
  Mold, *255*, 256–57

Cola Chicken Wings, 86, *87*
 Preserved, Grilled Squid with, 222,
  223
Lettuce
 BLT Fried Rice, 140, *141*
 Fried Fish, Tomato (FFLT) Sand-
  wich, *220*, 221
 Hot Salad, *112*, 113
Lo Bak Go, Crispy Ham and Cheese,
 118–19, *119*
Lobster Cantonese, *231*, 232–35
Lo Mai Fan
 Roasted Mushroom, 152–53, *153*
 XO Seafood, 154–55, *155*
Lychees
 Mini Sweet-and-Sour Meat Loaves,
  202, 203

M

Mac Soup Mac Salad, *160*, 161
Malted Chocolate Waffles, 58, *59*
Maple Candied Bacon, Nam Yu,
 54, *55*
Meat. *See* Beef; Pork
Meat Loaves, Mini Sweet-and-Sour,
 202, 203
Milk
 evaporated, about, 18
 Iced Black Sesame, *72*, 73
 Soy, 70, *71*
 sweetened condensed, about, 25
 Tea, 74
 Tea, Coffee, 74, *75*
Milk Bread
 Blankets, Scallion, Piggies in,
  96–97, *97*
 Buns with Butter, 60–61, *61*
MSG, about, 15, 21
MSG Caramel Dipper, 240
Mushroom(s)
 dried shiitake, about, 17
 Roasted, Lo Mai Fan, 152–53, *153*
Mustard
 Chinese Hot, *27*, 30
 powder, hot, about, 21
Mustard greens, pickled
 about, 22
 Green Chili Ginger Scallion Sauce,
  27, 31

INDEX 269

N

Nam Yu Maple Candied Bacon, 54, *55*
Noodle(s)
    Beef Brisket Soup, 182–83, *183*
    Beef Chow Fun, *178*, 179–80
    Buttery Oyster Sauce, 158, *159*
    Crispy Sheet Pan Fried, *165*, 166–67
    Steamed Garlic Prawns over Mung
        Bean Vermicelli, *168*, 169
    XO Cheung Fun, 176, *177*
Nut milk bag, 40
Nuts
    Fish Mix, *80*, 81
    Shrimp and Walnuts (Hup To Ha),
        228–29, *230*
    Steamed Sponge Cake with Orange
        and Almond, *258*, 259–60

O

Oil, Shrimp Chili, *33*, 36
Oils, 22
Onions, green. *See* Scallion(s)
Orange and Almond, Steamed Sponge
    Cake with, *258*, 259–60
Oyster Sauce
    about, 22
    Noodles, Buttery, 158, *159*

P

Panzanella, Yauh Ja Gwai, 110, *111*
Pasta. *See also* Noodle(s)
    Buttery Oyster Sauce Noodles, 158,
        159
    Cantonese Minestrone, 128–29, *129*
pasta (cont.)
    Fuyu Cacio e Pepe Mein, 162–63, *164*
    Mac Soup Mac Salad, *160*, 161
Peanuts
    Fish Mix, *80*, 81
Peanutty-Chili Sauce, Wontons in a, 172
Peppers. *See* Chili
Pickled mustard greens
    about, 22
    Green Chili Ginger Scallion Sauce,
        27, 31

Piggies in Scallion Milk Bread Blan-
    kets, 96–97, *97*
Plastic wrap, 40
Pomegranate Molasses Cha Siu,
    212–14, *213*
Popcorn, Stovetop Salt and Pepper, 78, *79*
Pork. *See also* Bacon; Ham; Sausage
    and Chive Dumplings with Caramel-
        ized Onion Soy Butter, *92–93*, 94–95
    Ham Yue Yook Beng Stuffed Cabbage,
        189, *190*
    Lobster Cantonese, *231*, 232–35
    Mini Sweet-and-Sour Meat Loaves,
        202, 203
    Patty, Steamed, with Salted Fish
        (Ham Yue Yook Beng), 188–89, *189*
    Pomegranate Molasses Cha Siu,
        212–14, *213*
    Schnitzel, Salt and Pepper, with Chi-
        nese Ranch, 186–87, *187*
    and Shrimp Wonton Soup, 170–72, *171*
Potato(es)
    Coconut Taro Sago Dessert Soup,
        242, *243*
    Sweet, Curry Potpie, 194–95, *196*
    Taro Root Diner Hash Browns with
        Sweet-and-Spicy Ketchup, 56, *57*
Potpie, Sweet Potato Curry, 194–95, *196*
Prawns, Steamed Garlic, over Mung
    Bean Vermicelli, *168*, 169

R

Radish, salted, about, 22
Rice
    Clay Pot (Without a Clay Pot), *149*,
        150–51
    Congee Arancini, 146–47, *148*
    cooking guide, 133–34
    Fried, BLT, 140, *141*
    Fried, Canned Corn and Scallion,
        138, 139
    for fried rice, preparing, 134
    Ginger Congee, *142*, 143
    long-grain jasmine, about, 133
    Roasted Mushroom Lo Mai Fan,
        152–53, *153*
    Rotisserie Chicken Congee, 144, *145*
    short-grain glutinous sticky, about, 133
    Steamed, The Perfect Pot of, Without
        a Rice Cooker, 136, *137*
    tea, preparing, 136
    XO Seafood Lo Mai Fan, 154–55, *155*

Rice noodles
    Beef Brisket Noodle Soup, 182–83, *183*
    Beef Chow Fun, *178*, 179–80
    XO Cheung Fun, 176, *177*

S

Sago Taro Coconut Dessert Soup, 242, *243*
Salads
    Cabbage, with Fried Garlic Sesame
        Dressing, *108*, 109
    Hot, *112*, 113
    Mac Soup Mac, *160*, 161
    Yauh Ja Gwai Panzanella, 110, *111*
Salt, 15
Salt and Pepper Seasoning, *32*, 34
Salted preserved fish. *See* Ham Yue
Salted radish, about, 22
Sandwiches
    Fried Fish, Lettuce, Tomato (FFLT),
        220, 221
    Steamed Then Fried Egg, *63*, 64–65
Sauces
    Black Bean Garlic, *26*, 28
    Green Chili Ginger Scallion, *27*, 31
    Salty, Malty Ovaltine Hot Fudge, *250*, 251
    store-bought, 17–25
    XO, *33*, 37
Sausage
    Chinese (lap cheong), about, 17
    Clams Casino, 224–25, *225*
    Clay Pot Rice (Without a Clay Pot),
        149, 150–51
    XO Seafood Lo Mai Fan, 154–55, *155*
Scale, digital, 40
Scallion(s)
    and Canned Corn Fried Rice, *138*, 139
    in Cantonese cooking, 14
    Green Chili Ginger Sauce, *27*, 31
    Milk Bread Blankets, Piggies in, 96–97, *97*
    Sizzling Steamed Fish with Seasoned
        Soy Sauce, 218, *219*
    Sour Cream and Green Onion Dip,
        106, *107*
    XO Cheung Fun, 176, *177*
    XO Sauce, *33*, 37
Scallops
    Corn Chowder, 126, *127*
    dried, about, 17
    XO Seafood Lo Mai Fan, 154–55, *155*
Seafood. *See also* Anchovies; Shrimp
    Clams Casino, 224–25, *225*
    Corn Chowder, 126, *127*

dried, types of, 17
dried scallops, about, 17
FFLT (Fried Fish, Lettuce, Tomato) Sandwich, 220, 221
Grilled Squid with Preserved Lemon, 222, 223
Lobster Cantonese, 231, 232–35
Lo Mai Fan, XO, 154–55, 155
Sizzling Steamed Fish with Seasoned Soy Sauce, 218, 219
Steamed Garlic Prawns over Mung Bean Vermicelli, 168, 169
Tinned Dace Dip, 84, 85
Seasoned Soy Sauce, 32, 35
Seasoned Soy Sauce, Sizzling Steamed Fish with, 218, 219
Seasoning, Salt and Pepper, 32, 34
Sesame seeds
    Iced Black Sesame Milk, 72, 73
    Milk Bread Buns with Butter, 60–61, 61
    Toasted Sesame Shortbread, 244–45, 246
Shallots, fried, about, 18
Shaoxing wine, about, 22
Shortbread, Toasted Sesame, 244–45, 246
Shrimp
    Chili Oil, 33, 36
    Cocktail with Fuyu Chive Aioli and Gingery Cocktail Sauce, 90, 91
    Crispy Sheet Pan Fried Noodles, 165, 166–67
    dried, about, 17
    Fish Mix, 80, 81
    paste, about, 25
    Paste Butter, Charred Cabbage with, 114, 115
    and Pork Wonton Soup, 170–72, 171
    Steamed Garlic Prawns over Mung Bean Vermicelli, 168, 169
    Sticks with Ginger-Scallion Tartar Sauce, 88–89, 89
    and Walnuts (Hup To Ha), 228–29, 230
    XO Sauce, 33, 37
    XO Seafood Lo Mai Fan, 154–55, 155
Skillets, 39
Soups
    Beef Brisket Noodle, 182–83, 183
    Cantonese Minestrone, 128–29, 129
    Coconut Taro Sago Dessert, 242, 243
    Corn Chowder, 126, 127
Sour Cream and Green Onion Dip, 106, 107
Soybeans, black. See Fermented black soybeans
Soy Milk, 70, 71
Soy Sauce
    light and dark, about, 21

Seasoned, 32, 35
Seasoned, Sizzling Steamed Fish with, 218, 219
Spam
    Mac Soup Mac Salad, 160, 161
    Steamed Then Fried Egg Sandwich, 63, 64–65
Squid, Grilled, with Preserved Lemon, 222, 223
Stainless-steel steaming tray, 40
Steamer, setting up a, 43
Steaming rack, 40
Steaming tray, 40
Strainer, fine-mesh, 40
Sugar, 15
Sundae, Salty, Malty Hot Fudge, 250, 251
Sweetened condensed milk, about, 25
Sweet Potato
    Coconut Taro Sago Dessert Soup, 242, 243
    Curry Potpie, 194–95, 196

Taro
    Diner Hash Browns with Sweet-and-Spicy Ketchup, 56, 57
    Sago Coconut Dessert Soup, 242, 243
Tea
    Coffee Milk, 74, 75
    Eggs, Jammy Marble, 82, 83
    Milk, 74
    No-Churn Yuen Yeung Ice Cream Cake, 247, 248–49
    rice, preparing, 136
Thermometer, 39
Tinned dace fish
    about, 25
    Tinned Dace Dip, 84, 85
Toasted sesame oil
    about, 25
    Toasted Sesame Shortbread, 244–45, 246
Tofu
    Cabbage Salad with Fried Garlic Sesame Dressing, 108, 109
    Crispy Sheet Pan Fried Noodles, 165, 166–67
    Steamed Silken, with Beefy Black Bean Garlic Sauce, 200, 201
Tomato(es)
    BLT Fried Rice, 140, 141
    Fried Fish, Lettuce (FFLT) Sandwich, 220, 221

Vinegary, Marinated, Steamed Egg Custard with, 122–24, 125
Yauh Ja Gwai Panzanella, 110, 111

Vegetables. See also specific vegetables
    Cantonese, guide to, 104–5
    Chinatown Crudités with Sour Cream and Green Onion Dip, 106, 107
    Crispy Sheet Pan Fried Noodles, 165, 166–67

Waffles, Malted Chocolate, 58, 59
Walnuts and Shrimp (Hup To Ha), 228–29, 230
White pepper
    about, 25
    Salt and Pepper Seasoning, 32, 34
Wine, Shaoxing, about, 22
Wok and wok ring, 40
Wontons
    in a Peanutty-Chili Sauce, 172
    Shrimp and Pork Soup, 170–72, 171

XO Cheung Fun, 176, 177
XO Sauce, 33, 37
XO Seafood Lo Mai Fan, 154–55, 155

Yauh Ja Gwai (Fried Cruller), 98–100, 99
Yauh Ja Gwai Panzanella, 110, 111
Yook Beng
    Ham Yue (Steamed Pork Patty with Salted Fish), 188–89, 189
    Ham Yue, Stuffed Cabbage, 189, 190
Yuen Yeung (Coffee Milk Tea), 74, 75
Yuen Yeung Ice Cream, No-Churn, Cake, 247, 248–49

Copyright © 2025 by Calvin Eng and Phoebe Melnick

Photographs copyright © 2025 by Alex Lau

Penguin Random House values and supports copyright. Copyright fuels creativity, encourages diverse voices, promotes free speech, and creates a vibrant culture. Thank you for buying an authorized edition of this book and for complying with copyright laws by not reproducing, scanning, or distributing any part of it in any form without permission. You are supporting writers and allowing Penguin Random House to continue to publish books for every reader. Please note that no part of this book may be used or reproduced in any manner for the purpose of training artificial intelligence technologies or systems.

Published in the United States by Clarkson Potter/Publishers, an imprint of the Crown Publishing Group, a division of Penguin Random House LLC, New York.
ClarksonPotter.com

CLARKSON POTTER is a trademark and POTTER with colophon is a registered trademark of Penguin Random House LLC.

Library of Congress Cataloging-in-Publication Data
Names: Eng, Calvin, author. | Melnick, Phoebe, author. |
   Lau, Alex, photographer. Title: Salt Sugar MSG: Recipes
   and Stories from a Cantonese American Home / by
   Calvin Eng with Phoebe Melnick; photographs by
   Alex Lau. Identifiers: LCCN 2024012059 (print) | LCCN
   2024012060 (ebook) | ISBN 9780593582084 (hardcover) |
   ISBN 9780593582091 (ebook) Subjects: LCSH: Bonnie's
   Restaurant | Cooking, Chinese. | LCGFT: Cookbooks.
Classification: LCC TX724.5.C5 E64 2025 (print) | LCC
   TX724.5.C5 (ebook) | DDC 641.5951—dc23/eng/20240328
LC record available at https://lccn.loc.gov/2024012059
LC ebook record available at https://lccn.loc.gov/2024012060

ISBN 978-0-593-58208-4
Ebook ISBN 978-0-593-58209-1

Printed in Malaysia

Editor: Jennifer Sit
Editorial assistant: Elaine Hennig
Designer: Robert Diaz
Production editor: Natalie Blachere
Production manager: Jessica Heim
Compositor: Merri Ann Morrell
Food stylist: Tyna Hoang
Food stylist assistant: Alyssa Kondracki
Prop stylist: Nicole Louie
Prop stylist assistant: Taylor Bittenbender
   and Olivia King
Copyeditor: Sharon Silva
Proofreaders: Andrea Connolly Peabbles, Erin Roll,
   and Lisa Lawley
Indexer: Elizabeth Parson
Publicist: Lauren Chung
Marketer: Monica Stanton

10 9 8 7 6 5 4 3 2 1

First Edition

Clarkson Potter/Publishers
New York
clarksonpotter.com

Cover design: **ROBERT DIAZ**
Cover photographs: ALEX LAU